Advance Praise for *Profit Motive*

"*Profit Motive* is a must-read book that guides readers through one of the most fundamental foundations of leadership—understanding the motivations driving the world around us."
—Governor Jeb Bush

"What Charles is talking about in this book, *Profit Motive*, is how to work smart. That is a pretty good start to making your first billion."
—T. Boone Pickens, Founder, Chairman and CEO at
BP Capital and TBP Investments Management and
author of *New York Times* best seller *The First Billion Is the Hardest*

"Charles Sauer's *Profit Motive* is the Ronald Reagan of economics books."
—Grover Norquist, president of Americans for Tax Reform

"*Profit Motive*, by Charles Sauer, is a compelling read that conveys an idea common to economists. People and businesses are profit-seeking. Put out a bread crumb trail of incentives—profit—and it will be followed."
—John C. Goodman, President of the Goodman Institute for
Public Policy Research and the "Father of Health Savings Accounts"

"*Profit Motive* is a must-read for someone on both the political right and left. On the left, we need to understand how a radical like Charles Sauer views the world, and on the right . . . well you all can do what you want."
—Thom Hartmann, nationally syndicated radio show host
Four-time winner of Project-Censored Award,
New York Times best-selling author

"Profit isn't a four letter word. Thanks to Charles Sauer for reminding us of that."
—Stephen Moore, former senior economics writer for the
Wall Street Journal and former member of the *Journal's* editorial board.
He was also founder of the Club for Growth and
author of numerous popular books.

"In *Profit Motive*, Charles Sauer channels Milton Friedman, showing that self-interest, broadly defined, rules our every behavior and collective outcomes."

—**Laurence J. Kotlikoff,** William Fairfield Warren Distinguished Professor and professor of economics at Boston University, *New York Times* best-selling author

PROFIT
MOTIVE

PROFIT MOTIVE

What Drives the Things We Do

Charles Sauer

SelectBooks, Inc.
New York

This edition published by SelectBooks, Inc.
For information address SelectBooks, Inc., New York, New York.

First Edition

ISBN 978-1-59079-444-9

Library of Congress Cataloging-in-Publication Data

Names: Sauer, Charles D., author.
Title: Profit motive : what drives the things we do / Charles Sauer.
Description: First Edition. | New York : SelectBooks, Inc., [2018] |
Includes
  bibliographical references and index.
Identifiers: LCCN 2017020724 | ISBN 9781590794449 (hardbound book : alk.
  paper)
Subjects: LCSH: Profit. | Organizational behavior. | Motivation (Psychology)
Classification: LCC HB601 .S24 2018 | DDC 338.5--dc23 LC record available at
https://lccn.loc.gov/2017020724

Book design by Janice Benight

Manufactured in the United States of America
10 9 8 7 6 5 4 3 2 1

This book is dedicated to my father.
He taught me to think. He taught me to love life.
He taught me to love people and to cherish every conversation.
And he taught me to love writing.
I wish that he were around to read this book,
because it wouldn't have been possible without him.

CONTENTS

Foreword

Throughout *Profit Motive*, Charles Sauer explains in an engaging way something that is a cornerstone to dealing with people. People are motivated by incentives. Charles calls that incentive gaining a "Profit."

Understanding Charles's concept of "Profit Motive" is one of foundations that can be used to run a successful business, be an effective leader, and just make it through everyday life intact—or perhaps even successfully. As one example, in an early section Charles demonstrates how understanding the profit motives of your car dealer can make your next car purchase a much better experience.

Incentives aren't always financial though, so Charles also makes it clear that gaining a "profit" isn't always about money. In fact, the profit or incentive people react to can be many things besides financial reward. The incentive might be both practical and meet a strong desire, such as arranging a work schedule that allows more time with your family. Or "the profit" could be an opportunity to take on greater responsibility to boost your career in the long run, or a referral to a mentoring program to increase skills that can lead to a more powerful position or gaining more respect.

The point that Charles is making is something that I have employed in my career to help lead people. At the early stages of starting a company, it is just you and an idea. The success of an entrepreneur often relies on convincing others to follow you on that journey. That can be based on dreams of wealth. I have promised briefcases of money to people (and delivered on that promise). That can also be promising an inclusive workplace—I have done that, too. Each person is different, but they all have some motivation.

I might not agree with all of Charles's political views or con-clusions, but I agree with his main point that understanding how people are motivated and working from that foundation would be a benefit to us all. And, the way that he makes this point, and the creation of his "Profit Man" to further help readers walk through profit motives makes *Profit Motive* a must read.

By making his point through interviews and his character "Profit Man" Charles effectively makes the case that if you can identify your own profit motives, and if you can identify the profit motives of others and leverage these motivations, you are more likely to achieve your goals.

Charles aims to provide readers with a method to increase success in many areas. If you follow his advice to observe the world around you to identify people's profit motives, it's likely you'll first find these motivations in business decisions that you did not recognize in the past. In fact, this could be what you need right now to identify a new business idea or opportunity. Or understanding this principle might help you to enjoy greater success at your current company.

Also, understanding people's motivations to profit can be use-ful in the other parts of our life. Charles shows how an under-standing of what drives people applies to the goals we have for our relationships with our partner and children and to what we hope to gain from our government or political and religious insti-tutions—and how it is key to making good choices for important things like health care options.

Charles starts and ends his book with a thought experiment. I like that idea, so here goes: What amount of profit could you lose by learning a new principle for success? And what amount of profit do you stand to gain from learning this new principle? So, what is the potential percentage of profit gained?

In other words, read *Profit Motive*.

—Doug Humphrey
Cofounder of Digex and internet pioneer

Acknowledgments

THANK YOU TO MY WIFE AND KIDS for their support during my writing of *Profit Motive*. It was both a time and mental commitment, and they were supportive and understanding through the entire process. Thanks to Nancy Sugihara, the editor, for her patience, thoroughness, and ideas that fully helped shape the book into a finished product.

And thank you also to the illustrator Max Espinoza for drawing Mr. Profit Man according to my idea to adapt a cartoon based on Fredrick Burr Opper's famous political cartoons of late nineteenth century industrialists. Opper's caricatures were intended to villainize the industrialists, but we wanted something different, and Mr. Espinoza pulled it off well. In our updated rendering of an Opper caricature, Profit Man doesn't seem lovable at first, but Max expertly allows Profit Man to appear more friendly as you get to know him throughout the book, and his trustworthiness and loyalty shine.

1

What Does Profit Motive Really Mean?

LET'S START OFF WITH A QUICK thought experiment. If an architect is getting paid to design a building and his company also produces metric fasteners, like screws and bolts, is the architect likely to plan for standard connectors or ones that are metric?

The answer is of course metric, at least if that architect values his job. The employee is motivated to make decisions that benefit his company, and the company is motivated to maximize profit. This little thought experiment is multiplied in our lives hundreds, if not thousands, of times each day, and when each of our decisions are all added together and aggregated, they shape our lives. The reason that people make decisions one way or another is based on their Profit Motives. Almost every decision that we make is based on this principle of our motivation to profit, whether we think we will gain a financial benefit or another kind of benefit. So if we can better understand the profit motives of others we can use this information to our advantage.

The goal of this book is to reveal the underlying motivations of the world around us. Most people would agree to the obvious statement that *businesses are in business to profit*, but what does that really mean? In this book we look at different decisions that businesses make from pricing to employment choices, and even how seeking long-term profit can mean making decisions that at the time appear contrary to capitalist principles.

1

However, while our understanding of decision-making for a "for-profit" business is important, this book also goes beyond this to explore how "profit," or a valuable return, also drives decisions of nonprofit organizations, political movements, charities, churches, hospitals, think tanks, media, individuals, families, and the world around us. We need to ask why businesses or individuals make their decisions. We need to ask why certain people are in the news, why news sites run certain articles, or why businesses cultivate different cultures. Understanding the concept of Profit Motive helps provide the insight to answer these questions and provides a strong foundation to ask more questions.

Looking back, I realize that watching people I know struggle in the business world is what led me to write this book. I know plenty of people who have received top-notch educations but still fail to understand the world around them. Some of the reason is their lack of an inclusive business education. The schools they attended didn't teach much about selling, especially making sales with a focus on the person that they are selling to. But a major flaw of my friends' thinking is that they underestimate the Profit Motive of others.

Many who don't grasp the nature of Profit Motive seem to believe that people are good, and that in general most people go about their lives making rational decisions free from other coercions. And they are then often surprised when someone's "goodness" and making rational, "smart" decisions doesn't turn into business success. This is because business isn't about being good; business is about recognizing motivations and making sales. Businesses are motivated to profit. Furthermore, my friends and colleagues have often been motivated to do more "good" through their businesses than make a financial profit and are then surprised when the businesses don't develop as they thought they would.

It doesn't take a large investment of $1,000,000 to run into these problems; I speak to independent inventors all of the time who have invested a few hundred dollars into their idea and run into this same issue. An inventor may have solved a heinous problem—like the deaths of children left alone in overheated or freezing cars—but overlooks that in order for the idea to flourish somebody needs to buy the product for more than it would cost to manufacture it.

Watching these friends and their businesses flail around led me to look further into what makes others successful and examining the motivations behind their decisions. But it wasn't until I personally walked into this trap that I more fully understood the world around me.

I learned this when my grant submission to a major nonprofit organization was rejected. I realized that my submission should have been focused on *their* mission rather than on *my* organization's mission.

They were a nonprofit that "supported" organizations like mine, but it quickly became clear to me that my grant request had failed because they primarily looked out for themselves. I had been selling how good an investment my organization was (my motivation) instead of selling how my organization could further their mission (their motivation). They needed to justify spending to their donors, and selling my organization's mission wasn't going to accomplish that. Their donors gave money to support their own mission. I rewrote the proposal to focus on their mission and their goals, and the second one quickly moved through the process.

Was the nonprofit being greedy? Were they only being self-serving? Was "greed" really good like the line in *Wall Street*? Or is Ayn Rand's "selfishness" the driving force behind society?

As a culture we have been taught to look down on selfishness, but that also means that we often discount the selfish motivations of others. Personal selfishness isn't as important to recognize when others are acting in their own self-interest. (Spoiler: it's always this way.)

As an individual, you can be as giving and altruistic as you would like. But if you want to be more effective in how you give or more effective helping the people you're trying to help, this book will help you understand how other people have their own motivations. If you are just starting your career, understanding your company's and its leadership's profit motives will accelerate your career. If you run your own company, an understanding of Profit Motive will help you better understand your clients, customers, and employees. And, understanding profit motive will even help you manage your family better as you can quickly see each side of the relationship clearer.

Defining "Profit Motive"

To "profit" from something can be defined a lot of ways, so let's start with the simplest, least controversial ways from Merriam-Webster Collegiate Dictionary, 11th Edition:*

- to be of service or advantage: AVAIL
- to derive benefit: GAIN
- to make a profit

The second definition is the important one for our discussion of "Profit Motive" because, while money is very important, there is a lot more to profit than meets the eye. In fact, we will talk about this later in more depth, but only looking at profit as a static bank account can lead businesses and individuals in a bad direction very quickly. However, receiving benefits in our lives involves a lot of different things, including our money, family, health, power, knowledge, love, time, and countless other aspects of our lives. The primary idea is that people usually act in a way that benefits themselves in at least one of those ways. And the value that they

---

*It's a cliché, I admit—but it's still better than quoting from Wikipedia.

put on each of those variables is different and subjective to each person. So "profiting" is gaining an advantage or benefit.

Another variable we must consider is how an individual or organization values those benefits. The valuation of the variables is often subjective and depends on the individual or organization making the decisions. Some people, including some interviewed for this book, don't value money as highly as making a difference, winning, creating a new market, or some of the other variables mentioned above. On the other hand, organizations, both for-profit and nonprofit, have a singular drive toward financial gain. Financial profit drives companies so strongly that in many situations, if the leadership of a company isn't viewed as valuing those metrics enough, they are quickly replaced.

Therefore, everyone and every organization may be different. Two people may have the same benefits that they care about, but they might value them differently. Or, an organization might value big financial profits now and another organization might value higher profits in the long run. However, since a business must be active to stay in business, and an individual is active while he or she is alive, we all put value on things, and because of economizing behaviors (people tend to act in a rational manner) we tend to value things more that provide us more profit at a given time.

Therefore "Profit Motive" is my term for the idea that an acting organization, or individual, values things. Identifying those things and their relative value can help better understand or motivate that organization or individual.

To look at Profit Motive in real life, let's look at Facebook, the most popular social media platform in the world, which most of us use every day—for free. I use Facebook and I like Facebook. I also understand that I am not the client of Facebook. I am the product.

Facebook currently has more than a 1 billion active daily users and is the third busiest site on the internet.[1] It has hundreds of thousands of square feet of server farms, they have invested billions of dollars in their land and buildings, and they have installed billions of dollars of equipment into those buildings.

That is a lot of money just to give away a service for free.

What is Facebook's motive for giving away their service for free? What is their motivation to continue expanding their offering? Profit (of course). But since they aren't getting their profit from their 1 billion daily active users, where are they getting their profit? Ads and data. Facebook harvests incalculable amounts of personal information about its users which the users give away—in return for use of the site.

That means users of Facebook are almost like employees. Facebook wants to make sure that their employees are happy and that they continue to spend time, post pictures, register for events, and argue about politics and movies. But, at the end of the day, Facebook's real audience is their paying clients: the advertisers and data buyers. That motivation influences a lot of the company's decisions, but most importantly the privacy and data ownership policies of the site.

I smile every time that I see people post on Facebook, "This data is mine, and I don't give Facebook the right to use it." I imagine Facebook writing back, "Sure thing. Now go back to messaging your friend from high school to help our ads algorithm. Sincerely, the Zuck."

People do get value from Facebook. In fact, users of Facebook get enough value to give up their personal data (at least those who recognize they are giving up their data privacy). If we look a bit closer at the success of Facebook and the lack of support for competing platforms that charge membership fees, the value difference between data privacy and money becomes evident.

So Facebook users are the product and Facebook's Profit Motive isn't to serve them, but since users are the product and employee, they need to be happy because without them Facebook wouldn't have anything to sell. (Facebook may have 1 billion friends, but they also have a lot of competitors.) Everyone's profit needs and wants are fulfilled, and the Profit Motives are evident.

Another example of Profit Motive is membership at a country club. Country club memberships usually consist of two parts, an initiation fee and monthly dues. Most goods that we pay for tend to be priced at the same value that we get out of them. A Snickers bar is 99 cents because we get that value out of it, and if they charged more the buyers are likely to buy a competitor's bar. Country clubs are different. Country clubs usually provide a lot of services, including facilities for playing golf and tennis and provision of a restaurant and other nice areas for food and drinks. However, the price to join and monthly dues are often more, or many times more, than the value of the services that will be consumed.

If we look at this situation through the Profit Motive lens we can quickly understand why the price/value difference exists.

A club near me charges about $20,000 to join and $700 a month in dues. During the summer my family might be able to use the golf course enough to justify paying dues of $700 per month, but this is unlikely. There is a large portion of the year that we wouldn't be able to use the course at all, and we don't play tennis so we wouldn't even use all of the club's services. Maybe some of the food and drinks are free? Nope. We wouldn't come anywhere close to consuming the equivalent value of services compared to the dues that we would pay.

If the only products were those easily identified services—golf, tennis, and food—the country club could easily make more money by lowering their price to meet market demand. That would bring in more customers, and the revenue of the club would increase without a similar increase in overhead.

However, that isn't how a country club works. The true value of a country club is the exclusivity. Specifically, the exclusivity of the club is worth the difference between the market value of the services that you will consume and the price of the club. At least the membership values it this way. The bigger the difference, the assumption should be, the better the value of exclusivity.

There are two different groups that are each seeking, and each receiving, their own profits in this interaction. The country club is achieving the fullest profit by focusing on the wealthiest clients who demand their services. The club benefits because the more affluent members are likely to spend more money on luxury items and therefore spend more money at the club in total. The members are seeking the profit of less crowding, full access to amenities, and (the most valuable portion of the country club, its membership) the valuable network of people who can afford to pay for the luxury of the membership. The "valuable network" means having access to people that others can only dream of. In fact, the only reason that I, or my family, would consider joining a club is access to this exclusive group of people. One additional contract because of a relationship with another country club member can easily pay for the club membership, effectively making it an invaluable marketing tool instead of an additional entertainment expense.

Once again, though, it isn't all about money. A non-monetary version of Profit Motive is the basic training that military volunteers subject themselves to after enlisting in the military. The stress and physicality of basic training isn't necessary to obtain the strength and endurance that is required of any of the military branches. However, there are a lot of benefits to basic training that makes it worth it. The military branch profits by weeding out people who might not be cut out for the long-run demands of the jobs. The enlistee gains the benefit of knowing that his/her peers are making it through the same process and once they are through that all of their colleagues have been through the same training.

The definition of profit varies from person to person, but understanding their "Profit Motive" can help us understand the world around us and enable us to be more successful in getting what we want from others.

How to Use Our Knowledge of Profit Motive

The primary way to use our knowledge about "Profit Motive" should be to better understand the decisions and motivations of others. If you are paying attention to a company's or individual's Profit Motive, it is harder to be taken advantage of by scam artists. If you are paying attention to this, you might also be able to more easily close a deal. Or this might just provide a better understanding of the cronyism that drives much of our political world.

Another use of understanding Profit Motive is to leverage people's motivations to your advantage. One of my favorite examples of this is the ability to leverage college recruiters by understanding this concept. A college recruiter is normally paid by the college at least in part based on how many students they enroll. By providing a commission or bonus, the college has increased the willingness of the recruiter to persevere through the harder sells and work harder in general for their next recruit.

Just understanding that the recruiter makes money from signing up people is good information to have; it means they aren't an impartial judge, but instead more like a carnival barker attempting to bring you into the tent. They are selling something, and the bigger their bonus the harder the sales pitch is going to be.

However, if you're applying to colleges, why not leverage this situation and make the carnival barker work for you?

The college is the one paying the recruiter, but there is a fairly easy way to make it look like the money is in your pocket. Just tell the recruiter that you want to go to their college. Then you hold the money. You and your eager signature are the only thing standing between them and their increased pay check. Now you can push for more scholarships and for the best and least expensive housing. You can push for extra money for books, or even a guarantee that certain classes will be offered. The question is what *can't* you ask for? Just tell the recruiter that you are ready to sign on the dotted line, but you need something (and be explicit about that something). At the very least you have tried, but more than likely the recruiter is now going to work for you. You have now given them the motivation to work to make you happy. You have identified the motivation and used it to your advantage.

This example is just the start. If the commission is large enough, as it is on car sales, the same motivations are in play. If fact, car dealers are fairly used to this method, so they have introduced layers of "Yes." And each layer is designed for them for better selling.

The next time you walk into a car dealership, look around and take in the situation. A car dealership is designed to sell. And part of that design is to take away the leverage of the buyer, unlike a casino that has all of the odds in their favor. On a car lot the odds should lie with the buyer. They have the money, which should put them in control, but the car dealership wants to flip those odds so they can make more sales.

One strategy that dealerships use is to "layer the sale"—and each layer is designed to remove leverage. Most dealerships have at least two layers to a sale, and some have many more, so let's focus on the primary two and see how Profit Motive applies.

Layer one, the guy that first has contact with you, is the salesperson. His goal is to get to know you, understand what you are looking for (or convince you to look for something), and then guide you through the lot and eventually toward a car. So far there's no harm, no foul. Someone is shopping for a car, and the salesperson is helping them. All of the profit motives seem fairly obvious, and everything still appears like the college recruitment scenario.

Then, after the test drive and some practiced chitchat, you end up back at the salesperson's desk to discuss price. This is when the de-leveraging starts, at least for the buyer because a car dealer's goal is to now put themselves in the driver's seat. Once you say that you would like to discuss price, suddenly a new anonymous person is introduced into the conversation. Every dealership has a different name for the person, but this is who your original contact person walks over to in order to discuss price.

The dealership has this next layer precisely because of the same reasons given in the previous college recruiter example. You can move the first salesperson to your side, but an anonymous guy you haven't met is a lot harder to have contact with. Additionally, the job of the first salesperson is to sound like he is actually on your team now (that is why he built up the relationship and emotional connection with you through his chatting). You might actually have the him on your side, but the other reason for the dealership to add in the third party is to give the salesman someone to blame—a scapegoat—for not meeting all of your demands.

Let's assume that you make it through this first layer of sales, and you have gotten everything that you wanted. The last time I bought a car I did accomplish this. However, I got hung up on the second layer.

This happened because after the price is agreed to, it's time to fill out the "paperwork." Somehow, and this is definitely planned, the paper work with the next person at the dealership is also accompanied by more sales pitches about both the varieties of financing and the high margin add-ons to the purchase that you already agreed to. Car dealerships make money on cars like gas stations make money on gas; these places make a higher margin when you buy the candy that they sell, whether this is Mike and Ike treats or "free" oil changes.

By getting you past the first layer of negotiations the dealership now feels in control in this second stage, and buyers can easily spend another $1–2 thousand dollars, especially when these costs can be calculated by merely adding them into the financing, which can make the amounts appear smaller. For example, adding a full-service maintenance plan, the "VIP" maintenance plan, might cost $2,000 but only add an additional $30 per month into the payment.

The goal, their Profit Motive, throughout the process isn't to make a killing by any means possible, but to achieve sales and "return sales." The dealership also wants you to come back. However, since almost all of their business is based on negotiations, car dealerships have taken great care to ensure that the balance of power tips in their favor. They have ensured the profit motive of the buyer is met by making them feel that they got a good value and at the same time that their own profit motive was maximized as well.

If you are wondering how to reduce the dealership's ability to maximize their profit, the answer is that you must always be willing to walk out. You also need to know that every time you say "yes" you should be asking for something more in return for that "yes."

Both of these examples are of leveraging Profit Motive, but the most important use of this book is to provide a better understanding of the world around you.

Take one of the more jarring examples of people's Profit Motive. Even churches need to consider profit when making decisions. If the leader of the church wants to alter their direction, what is that going to mean to the donors, tithers, and the future of the church? Pastors, fathers, preachers, and clerics all need a basic understanding of the need to profit in order to run a sustainable church.

A lot of us understand the basic principle that a church needs money to survive, but many of us fail to apply that knowledge. If a church is in business to profit, how are they implementing their selling? Are they just pandering? Or does their need to continue to profit mean that churches feel they should maintain a more conservative stance despite having liberal young parishioners because many of the current supporters/donors are older? Is the church as effective as their donors think they are? When we buy a Snickers bar we know the quality of the bar when we eat it, but when we donate to something, we receive some value from doing this, but don't necessarily get back the full value of our donation. The organization that receives the donation usually provides the bulk of the value of donations to someone besides the original donor. And, the person, or people, that receive the benefit aren't the ones paying for it. It's like the Riddler from Batman: When is a client not the client?

To put it another way: in a charitable transaction it is like a customer entering a convenience store and paying for a Snickers bar, but unlike a normal situation where the cashier would then hand the bar back to the purchaser, when a donation is made, it is like the cashier is handing the bar to someone else in line. Normally, the buyer of a Snickers bar would care about taste, size, freshness, and price. However, when they no longer receive the full benefit from their purchase they no longer will be able to judge anything about it except the "price." That is not how almost any normal business is run, and it can lead to sales pitches that often deviate from the reality of the assistance requested.

The client/consumer difference doesn't mean that profit is bad or that a church should adopt a fundraising strategy that promises to bankrupt them, and it doesn't mean that business owners or leaders of nonprofit organizations need to be bad people to earn a profit. What it does mean is that when a business or a nonprofit hires someone, they are not performing a charitable action, or when they set their pricing or ask for a donation of a certain amount they are not setting it for any reason other than to maximize profit.

Maximizing profit, especially financial profit, is an important and primary driver for many organizations, but, again, an understanding of what this drive means in action can help to provide us with a better understanding of the economy. And, in some cases, understanding the Profit Motive can help us explain—and maybe figure out a solution for a problem or identify an opportunity for improving a situation—even for things like racism or sexism in the marketplace. For instance, opening up entrepreneurship opportunities for women in primarily male-dominated societies has created many circumstances where men are reliant on a paycheck provided to them by a female business owner. That relationship or profit seeking can tear down age-old cultural barriers faster and more sustainably than a government edict can. And that is just one example.

As Uri Gneezy and John List point out in their book *The Why Axis: Hidden Motives and the Undiscovered Economics of Everyday Life*, problems of racism and discrimination are more likely to be solved by looking at the economic incentives of people and companies to increase profits than examining prejudice in society in general.

An economic explanation doesn't make racism right, but when we understand the motivations behind some of these marketing decisions it becomes easier to address them by a method, whether it is public policy, public awareness, or entrepreneurial solutions.

Profit Motive is everywhere when you are watching for it. The effects of incentives and motivations are all around us, and a better understanding of how the profit-driven motivations affect us is beneficial.

Ayn Rand's Theology

Economists often discuss incentives, but we rarely discuss "motivations." However, incentives work and fail because of correctly or incorrectly identifying and targeting motivations. In *Profit Motive*, I identify the primary economic motivation of individuals as well as also discussing what drives businesses, nonprofits, media, families, and the world around us is "Profit."

Some might read "profit" and read "greed" or "selfishness," and that often isn't very far off from the truth, but unlike Ayn Rand I don't assert that selfishness is necessarily a virtue. The point of this book is that "other" people act in their own self-interest and that an active mind that recognizes that can better understand the world and actions and act in a way—whether this is altruistic or self-interested—that best meets their ends.

However, before we start it is important to understand what Ayn Rand said about selfishness in the introduction to one of her defining books of a collection of essays, *The Virtue of Selfishness*:

> The Objectivist ethics holds that the actor must always be the beneficiary of his action and that man must act for his own rational self-interest. But his right to do so is derived from his nature as man and from the function of moral values in human life—and, therefore, is applicable only in the context of a rational, objectively demonstrated and validated code of moral principles which define and determine his actual self-interest. It is not a license "to do as he pleases" and it is not applicable to the altruists' image of a "selfish" brute nor to any man motivated by irrational emotions, feelings, urges, wishes or whims.
>
> This is said as a warning against the kind of "Nietzschean egoists" who, in fact, are a product of the altruist morality and represent the other side of the altruist coin: the men who believe that any action, regardless of its nature, is good if it is intended for one's own benefit. Just as the satisfaction of the irrational desires of others is not a criterion of moral value, neither is the satisfaction of one's own irrational desires. Morality is not a contest of whims . . . .
>
> A similar type of error is committed by the man who declares that since man must be guided by his own independent judgment, any action he chooses to take is moral if he chooses it. One's own independent judgment is the means by which one must choose one's actions, but it is not a moral criterion nor a moral validation: only reference to a demonstrable principle can validate one's choices.
>
> Just as man cannot survive by any random means, but must discover and practice the principles which his survival requires, so man's self-interest cannot be determined by blind desires or random whims, but must be discovered and achieved by the guidance of rational principles. This

is why the Objectivist ethics is a morality of rational self-
interest—or of rational selfishness.

Since selfishness is "concern with one's own interests,"
the Objectivist ethics uses that concept in its exact and
purest sense. It is not a concept that one can surrender
to man's enemies, nor to the unthinking misconceptions,
distortions, prejudices and fears of the ignorant and the
irrational. The attack on "selfishness" is an attack on man's
self-esteem; to surrender one, is to surrender the other.[2]

Ayn Rand is adamant that selfishness is not immoral; rather
it is the moral duty of the individual to be selfish. When you start
applying the idea of "selfishness" to families and communities
and some of the decisions that we make every day, a support of her
theory begins to unravel. What doesn't unravel is that selfishness
exists. But because of her strong stance and rejection of any other
argument about the morality of following one's own self-interest,
many people have rejected her ideas from the outset.

As an economist, I don't feel that I have the authority to reject
Rand's assertion, but I also don't have the authority to fully accept
it. As an economist, I know what we can do is to look at the world
and attempt to explain how it works. We can look at the actions of
the market, the actions of the individual, and the actions of organizations. We can't judge their actions, in a moral sense, but we
can discuss their rationality and forecast future actions. Even then,
what I have noticed in the past is that what might not appear as
rational might in fact be a rational decision to the person making
that decision.

In other words, Ayn Rand is at least partially right, but to
look at the world and understand the decisions of others, and,
most importantly, forecast those decisions, we need to add in other
things like charity and altruism to more fully predict actions. We
can leave the lobbying to Ayn Rand about how those decisions
should be made and the morality of those decisions.

Econ Man vs. Profit Man

"Economic Man" or *homo economicus* is the name of a theory and actually was a dominant behavioral economic theory in the 1950s, 60s, and 70s. It posits that man acts in ways that are nearly perfectly rational. So if a Snickers bar is priced wrong, then Economic Man doesn't buy it. Economic Man is almost infallible. This is a bit of an overstatement, but the basic idea that permeated behavioral economics for thirty years was this idea of man.

The reason that I use the Snickers bar as an example is that the authors of *Nudge*, written by Cass Sunstein and Richard Thaler,[3] used the choice to buy a Snickers bar to show that Economic Man might not fully understand the decisions that he or she is making. They attempted to take apart Economic Man. They wanted to show that they could "Nudge" Economic Man into making certain decisions. Their "Nudge" theory is interesting, but they used Economic Man in way that it really shouldn't have been used and the years since the 1950s had largely proven that.

The theoretical Economic Man walking down the street doesn't exist, but taken in the aggregate, Economic Man does exist. For instance, the way to guess the number of Jelly Beans in the jar is to aggregate everyone else's guesses. People move rationally; they just might not all move rationally all of the time.

As we shall see, a Profit Man is no different. Not everyone makes 100 percent correct decisions that deliver the most profit to themselves. As I will discuss in more detail later, businesses often don't fully understand the profit choices before them; however, businesses believe that the choices they make will provide a profit, because a business isn't going to knowingly choose a path that will end up losing money. The same goes for employees in a company and individuals in a family.

Additionally, some of the irrationality around profit might also be a misunderstanding of a very rational choice to gain benefit. Later in the book is an interview I had with Thom Hartmann, who has a very successful radio and TV show. Before he started his TV show he was confronted with a decision about which channel to start on, and he chose a smaller channel rather than taking an opportunity with a large one. But on that small channel he was allowed to maintain the editorial control—which was a bigger area of profit for him and has worked out for him in the long run.

As in the case of Economic Man, Profit Man, is not perfect in his decision-making when every decision is inspected, and the point of the book is not to prove the existence of Profit Man, but to show that the assumption of the existence of Profit Man is a valuable and beneficial assumption.

Looking Ahead

Again, if you understand how profit drives others, you can then leverage that knowledge to make more money, build a better business, maintain a better relationship, or just understand why people do the things that they do, even the things that seem unbelievable.

We start this examination in chapter 2 by looking at the "Profit Motive" of companies. This is a section of life that most of us think that we understand, but when viewed through the economic lens of Profit Motive, some things that we think that we know become clear and others become blurry or even upside down. Capitalism seems like it might be almost completely profit driven, but it turns out that capitalism is more an art that relies on knowing what to value and when. Additionally, while capitalism itself is economically good, capitalists are at war, and that means that Profit Motive can lead them to places regarding competition that ideologues and theologians might fail to venture—including cronyism. It doesn't stop there, although prices are set based on Profit Motive, as is employment, start-up culture, and even investment.

All businesses have a lot of moving parts from clients and customers to employees. From branding and products to buildings and suppliers. The amount of decisions that are happening everyday can be overwhelming, but being able to understand a general direction to the answers of each of these questions is time and brain cycle saving advantage that can provide the advantage that you need to succeed.

It isn't just about making money, though, or is it? Later in chapter 6, I discuss the differences between for-profit and non-profit organizations. Nonprofits have those same issues clients/customers, branding, products, buildings, and suppliers. Just like their for-profit brothers, nonprofits live a world that is driven by Profit Motive. That isn't necessarily bad, it helps drive efficiency. However, the motives need to be acknowledged, by both the organizations leadership and the donors, in order of a nonprofit to serve their intended audience the most effectively. To look further into this phenomenon I interviewed recipients of donations from T. Boone Pickens to discuss his charitable efforts. We talked about how T. Boone Pickens so effectively builds wealth by understanding the motivations of the organizations he helps to build.

It was my personal experience with a nonprofit that sparked the idea for the "Profit Motive" and I still think that understanding the motivations and business side of a nonprofit is one of the best ways to fully understand the idea of Profit Motive in the world around us. Besides T. Boone Pickens, I look at well-known nonprofits, churches, and think tanks. (Spoiler: nonprofits aren't really "non" profit.)

Another market that we joke about being for sale, but rarely fully look into its profit aspects, is that of politics. While politicians are often skewered for their Profit Motives, it only ends up there because the cronies that lobby them, the fundraisers reliant on a percentage of their cut, the reality of their staff salaries and work load, and the other forces involved, are all contributing factors to their motives.

Capitol Hill is full of ideologues and ladder climbers, it consists of true believers and do-gooders as well as scum and cronies.

Like nonprofits, the problem in politics is that Profit Motive is often ignored, which gives undo leverage to the scum and cronies instead of empowering the ideologues and do-gooders. The problems are similar on both sides of the political aisle because the desks that members and staffers occupy are what stands between cronies and millions/billions of dollars. They are in the middle of a capitalist war and it is only if Profit Motive is acknowledged that they stand a chance.

In chapter 3 on the subject of politics, we talk with Capitol Hill staffers that have been my friends for years. We talk with top-level lobbyists, and we speak with the guy who might be the top politician on Capitol Hill: the Chairman of the House Rules Committee who sets the rules for every debate that happens on the House floor.

Building off the knowledge gained from looking at the motivations of businesses, nonprofits, and politics, it is time to talk about the media in chapter 4. The political Right usually talks about a vast Left-wing conspiracy controlling the media. However, is that true? Why might it look it that way? In this chapter I have the privilege of talking to a communications guy from the Left; a communications guy from the Right; an award-winning television show host from the right; and Thom Hartmann, a *New York Times* best-selling author, radio show host, and television show host from the far left.

It won't be a surprise that Profit Motive is a driving factor of the decisions that are made, but the answer about how "profit" does drive media is interesting. And the way that this Profit Motive shapes the stories that we hear and the way that media is delivered will hopefully be eye-opening.

It is also unsurprising that Profit Motive drives much of the next issue discussed in chapter 5 of the book, too. Health care is a huge industry that greatly impacts the federal budget and our personal budgets, but the way that Profit Motive works in this industry might surprise you. Don't worry, there is a lot of greed and a lot of bad. But what this chapter focuses on is a new and quickly growing market of affordable health care. Why did this market start, and now that it has started why is it growing slowly? The emergent free market movement in health care is like having a front row seat to an economic phenomenon that not many ever have the chance of witnessing.

In the discussion on health care, I get input from two free market pioneers and how Profit Motive shapes the current health-care market, why the two founders are different, what their Profit Motive is, and what they see for the future of health care in our country given the current market, incentives, and motivations.

While businesses and markets are shaped by Profit Motive, the most basic unit where this occurs is the individual, which I discuss in chapter 7. It is our own lives that are most affected and the place where most of profit-driven decisions are made. Making decisions about how we want to spend our money and how we want to spend our time and what our responsibilities are what we all deal with, but how we answer these questions is based on our individual Profit Motives. If that motivation has been considered, your answers can be thought through better and more effectively as well.

There are big questions that we answer in this discussion about individual "Profit Motives," but they might be best described by a conversation that I had with my three-old-girl before my wife went to a board meeting for her pre-school. My daughter wanted to know why her mom was attending a board meeting for her school. It was a good question, and the answer that I gave was that she cared about the school. However, there is really more to it. What was my wife's, and our, Profit Motive for her attending? The answer was that by being active in the school we become a super client, and by being active we can assure that our investment in the school is more valuable. By recognizing the "Profit Motive" of others we are possibly increasing the quality of education our daughter receives, and we are definitely increasing the accountability of the school and helping others while doing it. These types of actions we do and decisions we make are things that occur almost every day. Understanding where Profit Motive creeps in can help everyone take advantage of these moments as well.

We saved the best for last: Chapter 8 is about families. Profit Motive wouldn't be a real thing if it somehow ended at the threshold to your house. It doesn't. Little kids are the best at proving this, watch what happens if they throw something on the floor and you pick it up. They will almost throw it on the floor instantly every time. Why? Profit Motive. They want attention, they get attention, they do it again. If you can break this, by not giving them what they want, then parenting can become a lot easier. These secrets aren't a magic bullet. Kids are always going to test you, but an understanding of "Profit Motive" and that how it affects your kids, your spouse, and even your parents can be a significant tool to help you live a happier life.

In the family section, I interview my wife to see if she agrees with me. That was definitely a risk when it comes to my personal and familial "Profit Motive," but it was important for the book. In the end, her input helps make it clear that even in a marriage profits exist, and if we pay attention to those profits, family life can be better. My wife and I are a team, but we are also individuals with our own lives. That means that we I need to pay attention to her motives and her mine. In our marriage it isn't exactly like the motivation of a large corporation, but it is close enough that the similarities are very interesting.

After walking through the many ways that Profit Motive works and drives everyday decisions and actions, it should be easier to forecast what will happen in the fast-paced world around us, as well as see how a similar Profit Motive affects decisions at every point. After reading this book it should be easier to set your own goals and accomplish your own goals.

As you read these discussions, you should ask yourself about your own Profit Motives. Do they match those of your employers? Do your motives match the company you run? Does your wife understand your Profit Motives? Do you understand hers? These are all important questions, and hopefully as you better understand what Profit Motive is and how it effects the world around us you will be able to realize the full value of this book.

Profit Motive might not be the secret to understanding life, but a knowledge of it as provided in this book will help you get a lot closer to the answer.

2

Corporate Decision-Making

BUSINESS DECISIONS AREN'T LUCKY; business decisions aren't random. Businesses make decisions based on how they will provide a profit. Sometimes a company makes a decision to forego profits in the short run for larger profits in the long run, while others attempt to grow slow and steady. Some companies decide to pay their employees less, and some companies pay their employees more. Every decision that a business makes involves multiple variables and each business, business leader, and board attempts to account for all of the variables involved to make the long-run, profit-maximizing decision. Of course some make these choices better than others. At the most basic level, all of the decisions are being made to make a profit. While interacting with businesses as an individual, another business, or a public policy professional, an understanding of profit motives is vital.

To understand how a profit motive affects business decisions we will look at some of the most important and discussed variables, such as prices, taxes, cronyism, innovation, leadership, and employees. We will also look at how each of the decisions that a business makes might vary over the life of that business and how the same decisions can vary from business to business. This chapter is the product of years of relationships with people at every level of a business decision and the distillation of decades of experience of experts ranging from the small entrepreneur to the market economist and the groundbreaking innovator.

Profit seeking in business does not always bare its teeth as an ugly, greedy, monster; in fact, in the experience of talking to these experts it is often the opposite. Additionally, businesses, in the name of profit, are not always pro-free market. Sometimes what is best for a business, at least according to their experts, is less competition.

It is with a better understanding of the motives of business that individuals, policy makers, and other businesses can figure out how best to navigate life's everyday decisions.

Capitalism vs. Capitalist vs. Free Markets

Policies that respect and bolster economic freedom are pro-market, rather than pro-business. The distinction is important. A pro-business approach promotes policies that help specific businesses, such as the General Motors and Wall Street bailouts. Pro-market policies, on the other hand, focus on maintaining an open and fair competitive process, under which businesses can succeed or fail on their merits. As such, a policy agenda to help the poor involves removing obstacles to entrepreneurship for as many people as possible.[4]

—Ryan Young and Iain Murray
"The Rising Tide:
Answering the Right Questions in the Inequality Debate"

John D. Rockefeller made a fortune in oil. He didn't make that fortune by advocating for freer markets. To the contrary, John D. Rockefeller attempted to close off market access whenever he could. Rockefeller attempted to limit competition as much as possible in oil production, oil refining, transportation of oil, and even the retailing. John D. Rockefeller might be one of the best businessmen in the history of the United States, but he eschewed free markets at every turn, relying on market collusion with his competitors as well as government regulations and rules to control greater and greater portions of the oil industry.

Many free market advocates would frown upon his actions, but it is exactly his actions as a capitalist that drove his success. What the free market advocates miss is that free markets are fair, but capitalism is not a game with rules that promote "fairness." Capitalists aren't competing in a gentleman's game of golf—they are at economic war. In short, a good capitalist doesn't like competition because competition makes their path to success harder.

When Rockefeller was building his business, he didn't have the size to bully his way through the market. At that time the oil industry was new; oil derricks were everywhere and refiners were nearly as prevalent. There was so much oil, that was so cheap (compared to the market at the time) that refiners didn't care about waste. The rivers were so polluted that they went up in flames after waste from a refinery was lit on fire. Rockefeller saw that he could beat everyone else by limiting waste. He did this by selling more than three hundred by-products of the refining process and vertically integrating other parts of the business, including barrel production.

In one of my favorite stories about Rockefeller, he was walking through a factory and noticed that the barrels were being constructed with 40 drops of solder, and Rockefeller asked why they used that number. The factory experimented and eventually settled on 39 drops of solder, lowering the cost of barrel production and giving Rockefeller yet another competitive advantage.[5]

As Rockefeller's company grew, so did his influence over the market. He noticed that competitors would sometimes flood the market and lower the price of oil, and at other times it would spike. This was bad for the overall oil market, so among other pursuits, like the South Improvement Company, John D. Rockefeller worked on acquiring his competitors. The goal was to limit competition to prevent surprises in the market and reduce the ability of a startup oil company to out-innovate him.

Rockefeller didn't want a free market, but it can't be argued that Rockefeller wasn't a capitalist. He was—he might have been the best one. Many of today's largest businesses mimic Rockefeller's model and employ tactics that arbitrage actions by themselves as well as their competition.

The thing about capitalists is that they are greedy, they are self-serving, and they don't care about others unless it benefits them or their long-run business. This form of greed helps build an economy. Greed is also merely a symptom of Profit Motive in any economic system. Greed shouldn't be considered troubling, but it is important to know the type of person and the motivations of the market actors that we are talking about. In other words, don't ask a capitalist for their thoughts on a market and assume that you will get an answer that benefits the economy more than their company.

Cronyism

Later in his career Rockefeller decided that instead of fighting the government, he would attempt to work with the government. Of course his efforts often made it harder for other companies to compete with him, but for Rockefeller it was just part of the war. It could be argued that the collusion, kickbacks, and relentless acquiring of competitors is all free market, but when governments get involved, the free market ceases to exist and cronyism rules.

From Facebook to Google, large technology companies mimic Rockefeller's market-dominating technique of acquiring as many startups as they can in an attempt to identify the next trend and ward off competition before it takes market share away from them. However, like Rockefeller, they have also decided to use government policies, regulations, and courts to give themselves a step up on the competition. These are the actions of profit-seeking capitalism, but not the reactions or actions of a free market.

Capitalism works best with minimal amounts of government involvement. For instance, the government can help capitalists by enforcing property rights, but if that power extends to regulating what can be done on that land, government can restrict capitalism and economic growth. It is a minimal state of government control that best benefits capitalists that and can also provide the most free market. A free market allows for free entry and exit from a market—with no business licenses, zoning, user fees, and so forth.

In a state of minimal government regulation ideally everything works at its highest efficiency. Capitalists can enter and exit a competitive market filled by other capitalists driving economic growth. However, we don't live in a state of minimal government control. In fact, the government that we live with in the United States, changes the way that many markets function, resulting in markets that are anything but "free." While free markets disappear, capitalism and capitalists still exist, which quickly leads to cronyism.

Cronyism as I use it, is in the style that you might hear while walking the halls of Congress (the primary bastion of cronyism?). The word itself is used as a profanity there, and like any good profanity the definition changes or adapts based on the context and the inflection of the sentence. That can get a bit confusing, so let's discuss a few of the ways that I use "crony" and "cronyism."

First, we can start with the Merriam-Webster Collegiate Dictionary, 11th Edition definition, which is completely underwhelming and inadequate in this instance—except the fact that it is right next to "crook":

"Crony" is defined as "a close friend especially of long standing: PAL"

However, there is much more to cronyism than "friendship." In action, cronyism is often the leveraging of that friendship for financial gain. However, when it comes to cronyism, "friendship" is a fairly loose term, at least on Capitol Hill, but I have seen it elsewhere too, friendship can also be based completely on favors and money. On Capitol Hill this form of cronyism is the most egregious, because these relationships are often the result of a

Return-on-Investment calculation. Therefore, before the effort is put into developing the relationship someone has asked the question, "Can we make money from developing this relationship?" It makes complete sense, since profit motive is everywhere, but it is this type of relationship that can often be leveraged and managed in ways that drive public policy.

So, for the sake of this book—and if you work on Capitol Hill—a "crony" and "cronyism" are the leveraging of a relationship, usually a political relationship, to increase profit. Additionally, this leverage is usually needed because the "crony" or the crony's company is unable to compete with their competitors in an unregulated market, so their personal/corporate profit motive is to restrict the ability of their competitors to compete.

One example of cronyism in the wild is the 2012 passage of the American Invents Act. It was a bill that was ostensibly passed by retailers and mobile application developers to ward off "patent trolls." But the bill was heavily lobbied by large technology corporations that stood to gain from weakened patent rights. The problem for the proponents, or what gave away their crony pursuits, was that instead of attacking patent trolls, almost every provision in the bill merely weakened patent rights or made intellectual property more expensive to acquire and maintain. Even worse, many of the provisions actually made patent abuse easier.

One provision in particular was a statute passed by Congress in 2011 called AIA (Leahy-Smith America Invents Act). This changed the US patent system from First-to-Invent to First-to-File (While the provision was a so-called attempt to harmonize the US patent system with others around the world, the primary effect was to give large Research and Development companies a hand-up that left a giant chasm between the cost of intellectual property for the large corporation and the cost to the small garage inventor.

As a quick thought experiment, consider that if a company is paying a team of lawyers $1 million per year to file patents, and they file one hundred patents, each patent costs the company

$10,000. If on the other hand that same team of lawyers files only fifty patents, the cost-per-patent goes up to $20,000.

The same math was in place before AIA, but because of AIA the legal incentive was increased as well. Therefore, the goal for a large company is to get as many patents to the patent office as quickly as possible. This new incentive will likely lower patent quality and further swamp the US Patent and Trademark Office. These two outcomes were problems that the cronies trying to sell the bill said they were trying to fix, but they were pushed legislation that accomplished the opposite.

For the small inventor, it means that they now had yet another hurdle in front of them. Now they needed to rush to the patent office, but unlike the large research and development companies each patent cost the small inventor more money instead of less under the new system. First-to-File means that the garage inventor needs to move money that would have previously been used for marketing, development, sales, or research on a race to the patent office to beat the large company. Even worse, because the large companies have swamped the USPTO with lower quality patents, the patents filed by the small inventors will take even longer to process.

The patent reform fight has been an open battle of cronyism, but most cronyism isn't as overt. It is really more of a long-term game played out state-by-state and contract-by-contract.

Elon Musk is one of the capitalists who knows that he is in a war and has built a company prepared to fight each and every crony battle to give his businesses every advantage possible. He has created an aura of innovation around himself that helps protect his reputation for being inventive against his business activities, but he still has to run his business with the idea and motivation of profit as the primary factor. To do that, cronyism helps.

Musk's biggest ideas aren't exactly novel. The idea of electric cars has been around for years, as have solar panels and dreams of flying to Mars, but Musk's innovations on those ideas and enthusiastic approach to business has built excitement around his projects. His recent unveiling of the Tesla 3 has sold over 200,000 cars, and they might not even be ready for another couple of years. Like P.T. Barnum, standing on a soapbox barking at people to step right up to his circus, Musk has steadily drawn people into his imaginative world.[6]

The interesting thing is that many of the people paying for this circus have had no choice: taxpayers have long been funding Elon Musk's projects.

Taxpayers have shouldered the risk while Musk and his investors have profited many, many, times. Last year *LA Times* reporter Jerry Hirsch wrote that Musk's Empire is "fueled by $4.9 billion in government subsidies."[7] But his didn't come in the form of an oversized novelty check for $4.9 billion check written out to cash. Elon Musk's companies had to fight for every million.

In Texas, Musk's company SpaceX built a launch site, but only after playing hardball and receiving about $20 million[7] in economic development subsidies as well as other protections.[8] SpaceX has also benefited from Export Import bank loans, both indirectly (by US satellite manufacturers using them) and directly (by launching Israeli rockets).[9] The state of Nevada gave his company Tesla $1.3 billion in economic development incentives to build a battery plant near Reno, and, not be left out, SolarCity (Musk's creatively named solar panel company) capitalized on a tax credit covering 30 percent of the cost of installing their solar panels—totaling nearly half a billion in grants.

Even Sen. John McCain (R-Ariz.), who has long disapproved of earmarks, has been taken in by this modern carnival barker, tweeting compliments and courting Musk to bring his brand of entertainment to the Grand Canyon State.

Musk's companies aren't wrong for seeking this money or support from the people who hold the purse strings. That's just business. That is Profit Motive and what "Profit Man" should be expected to do. But the government shouldn't be picking winners and losers—It shouldn't be allowing cronies to sell them. Cronies don't care about fair competition; they don't want a fair market; they definitely don't want a fair fight. Cronies ask for things that benefit themselves, or ask for them for their companies for the sake of benefiting themselves. By subsidizing Musk's companies and allowing the will of the cronies to win the public policy fight, states and the federal government are harming innovation.

The problem with cronyism is that politicians are usually not businessmen and don't understand that Musk is in an economic war. Instead of banking on making customers happy, or what P.T. Barnum called "the noblest art," Musk seems to be have been taken by a more famous quote from Mr. Barnum: "There is a sucker born every minute." And like the rest of the world, Musk knows those suckers are concentrated in the US Congress and state legislative houses.

By pushing policies that support only one or two business, the country is losing out on many more growth opportunities from the next generation of innovators. The next best mousetrap might not be made because of the extra taxes paid to fund Elon Musk's $4.9 billion in government giveaways. The next startup might not move to Nevada because of the higher taxes to support Musk's battery factory. The next major US innovation might not happen because its inventor can't compete with multibillion dollar companies entrenched in the government's inner circles.

Businesses shouldn't be able to use politicians in this fashion. In fact, they should stand up and reject requests for subsidies. States should pursue public policy that promotes growth with low tax, business friendly policies. Instead, many states are pursuing policies that take from people already investing in the state, the ones responsible for paying for the economic development incentives. States should invest in policies that benefit all businesses, and the federal government should follow suit.

However, politicians aren't at war. (See chapter 3 for more on that.) Capitalists are at war. That means that capitalists are willing to use politicians, and politicians are often unaware that they are being used. Furthermore, politicians have their own Profit Motives and they are often seeking a kind of profit that capitalists can feed off of. The only solution is a very limited government that restricts the ways that capitalists can use politicians as weapons.

Pricing and Profit Motives

Every day we deal with prices. When we walk into grocery stores, convenience stores, or browse for that new Hawaiian shirt or 3D printer head on Amazon we are confronted with prices. As a father of three small girls, and also an economist, I am now fully aware that we aren't always aware of prices or value. An awareness of prices is something that we are both taught and that we grow into as we begin aggregating knowledge of different prices throughout our lives. And, sometimes despite a lifetime of experience with prices, we can still get price wrong. However, if society is taken as a whole we are pretty good at getting them right.

Prices are where the rubber hits the road for business attempting to maximize profit both in the short and long term. Pricing is one of the areas that helped solidify the idea of identifying a Profit Motive. Because it is where the rubber hits the road, it is also where a business exposes their profit strategy.

In a free and open market, a market with easy entry and easy exit, price is where the supply and demands curves intersect. If the price is above or below that intersection, a market will correct and adjust until the price is again at the intersection of supply and demand—the equilibrium point.

In some markets that we will discuss later the price is almost never at this intersection. In others, the price is deliberately set away from the equilibrium to create additional effects and because of other outside influences. Also, when government intervenes in a market with regulations and taxes, the equilibrium point can be harder to identify.

One place that almost everyone has been to and experienced a price that isn't at the equilibrium point is when going to the barber. The way barbers set the price is interesting. They have several factors that help frame their choice.

First, almost every man gets his hair cut at least once a month, and sometimes weekly, so men (and mothers) have a pretty reasonable understanding of the equilibrium point of a haircut. Second, barbers operate in a service industry and have historically been tipped for their service. Third, whatever a barber makes on the base price he is going to be taxed on. While all wages should be taxed, many people fail to claim tips, reducing their taxable income. Fourth, and final, people don't want to go out of their way to tip.

In my office building, like many office buildings, is a barber. He has been in business for more than fifty years. He knows hair, he works with his wife who knows hair, and other people that cut hair in Bob's shop know hair as well. They also know the reality that all four variables discussed above affect their asking price and that there is a "real" price equilibrium that they are trying to reach.

When I first visited this barber shop, I was busy finding out about the shop and the people instead of thinking about the price until the end of the haircut. After the trim I asked the owner how much I owed him and he said, "$16." That price point instantly signaled to me that I would be tipping between $1 to $4, and I ended up tipping $4.

They had set a price trap. I knew walking in that I was going to spend over $15 and under $25. In fact, I would say that my equilibrium price of a haircut is $18. So, if Bob charged more than that I would then be less likely to go back the next time I needed a haircut. I once got a haircut from a guy named LaRant in Washington, DC, and he charged me $50. It was a good haircut, but I haven't been back.

Back in my building, given his fifty years of experience, they probably have a pretty good understanding of the equilibrium price point. Therefore, their next goal is to maximize each barber's take home pay—as well as the shop's. They can do that by lowering the sales point and assuming that the tip makes up the rest. Now the shop needs to figure out how to maximize the tip. Since US currency comes in denominations of ones, fives, tens, and twenties (the relevant levels for this conversation), they have to decide what he thinks I will tip and how much effort I'm willing to go through to do it. By setting their haircuts at $16 they have made the decision that in most transactions they will need to give clients change of at least $4. If a barber averages a tip of $2 per haircut, he is at the equilibrium point, but for every dollar more he is beating the curve.

Additionally, let's consider the tax implications. If a barber is doing one hundred haircuts per week and four hundred per month and averaging $2 in tips for every cut, the barber is making $9,600 in tips. And assuming a 20 percent tax rate, Bob has increased his take-home pay, given the government involvement, by almost $2,000 and as much as $4,000 if his average tip was equal to the tip that I gave him. Taxes are necessary to fund government, but they also cause imperfections in the market.

Identifying imperfections like this, and how they change a market, can help market participants profit more than they would without market disturbance.

Another perfect example of this intervention, rightfully or wrongly, is the government's intervention in the tobacco industry. Governments, both federal and state, tax cigarettes heavily. These taxes distort the equilibrium price of cigarettes in a way that free markets could never do.

In a free market when tobacco company "A" competes with tobacco company "B" an equilibrium point will eventually be reached. As previously discussed, if company "A" or "B" raises their price the other company will gain market share. However, the government can intervene and raise the price across the board by implementing new taxes. This type of price increase in the case of cigarettes can be truly insidious. Tobacco is an addictive product, which means that the market is fairly inelastic. In other words, when the government raises prices across the board, very few people stop buying cigarettes. They are addicted to them. In a normal market the only way to engage in unfair pricing of an addictive product is to collude and price fix.

The government's intervention in the market is insidious for several reasons. First, the increased tax revenue is only possible by leveraging the addicted buyers. Second, the motive of the government for raising taxes doesn't take any of the business decisions or the profit calculations of the industry into account.

When it comes to the tobacco industry there are a lot of people who are indifferent toward, or even supportive of, the government actually breaking the industry. The government doesn't stop at single industries though; the government is everywhere, and anywhere that it distorts market prices there are real victims. Another case where the government distorts price and distorts the price equilibrium is in pharmaceuticals.

An example of the government getting caught distorting markets is the story of the indefensible Martin Shkreli. While the FDA attempted to vilify Shkreli for his price-raising tactics, the FDA also changed their approval rules to help stop companies like Martin Shkreli's Turing Pharmaceuticals, which became public enemy No. 1 overnight when it hiked the price of one drug from $13.50 per pill to $750. This was the FDA admitting that prices are market driven, and that when the government distorts market forces businesses can easily take advantage of the distortion to increase their profits. In fact, they might have a fiduciary responsibility to take advantage of the distortion if the short-term move doesn't change long-run profit outlook.

Martin Shkreli was called "evil,"[10] "opportunistic,"[11] and "capitalist"[12] when he raised the price of Daraprim from less than $20.00

a tablet to $750.00 a pill. This is often prescribed to HIV/AIDS patients, pregnant women, and babies for the treatment of Toxo-plasmosis, which for them is a life-threatening disease.[13] Granted, Shkreli is pretty much a terrible person, and not representative of most of the people in pharma; he's bad at business and likely very high on most people's Worst Person of the Year awards. Most peo-ple wouldn't want to do business with him, if only so they wouldn't have to look at his smug smirk. Those personality traits aren't some-thing that the FDA should need to change their procedures to cure.

Unlike the normal pharma-demagoguery that "patents cause high drug prices," Daraprim is a 62-year-old drug whose patents had run out a long time ago. The only hurdle left was the FDA. In order to bring a drug to market, the manufacturer needs to not only find out what's in the drug and how to produce it, but they also to go through the FDA's onerous approval process.

The FDA has two review levels, Standard and Priority. Stan-dard reviews have a "goal" of being finished in ten months. Pri-ority reviews, the FDA's version of the four-minute mile, have a "goal" of six months. That means that if everything goes com-pletely right, then after a generic pharmaceutical company has (1) identified a market opportunity, (2) figured out the recipe, and (3) the manufacturing process, the company now (4) has to sit on its hands and investment for six to ten months.

In Martin Shkreli's case, any entrepreneurial manufacturer that identified the new market created by the ridiculous 5,000 per-cent price increase of Daraprim, would have to sit on their busi-ness move as Turing Pharmaceuticals raked in the money while also putting people's lives at risk. That is to say, *the FDA was pre-venting competition that would force a lower price.*

Worse, any potential competing pharmaceutical companies would know that when they finally got to the end of the ten-month FDA slog, Shkreli and his smirk would be sitting there at the end ready to drop the price back down, since they already had the distribution channels figured out. Therefore, the FDA's quiet change was to move orphan drugs into the "Priority" review process instead of the "Standard" review process.

The long lag times between opportunities and distribution—in the Shkreli case the ten months to get an off-patent, orphan-drug to market—causes companies to make decisions that are bad for business. A broken down government-approval system is the biggest problem standing between patients and a functional market providing drugs at an affordable price, and it allows people like Martin Shkrelli to get away with robbery.

Price Gouging

While Shkreli's enormous and seemingly morally reprehensible price increase was motivated and made possible by inefficient government regulations, there are other times that the government stops price increases when they could, in fact, be beneficial to market efficiency.

In natural disasters and wars there are often dramatic and persistent supply shortages. Under normal market situations supply shortages would be accompanied by inversely proportional price increases. These price increases maintain the market equilibrium. But due to government intervention these price increases are often not allowed and even villainized as "price gouging."

When Superstorm Sandy hit the East Coast and ravaged New Jersey, business were hampered by pricing laws that wouldn't let them increase prices more than ten percent.

New Jersey's price controls, and the mocking of rational economic actors by politicians, increases irrational decisions and distorts markets at a time where a rational market could help save lives. It isn't just my heartless assertion; this is generally agreed on by all economists. In fact, when writing about the aftermath of Superstorm Sandy, Matthew Iglesias, a left-leaning economist, said in Slate, "Stopping price hikes during disasters may sound like a way to help people, but all it does is exacerbate shortages and complicate preparedness."

And he goes on to say:

> The basic imperative to allocate goods efficiently doesn't vanish in a storm or other crisis. If anything, it becomes more important. And price controls in an emergency have the same results as they do any other time: They lead to shortages and overconsumption. Letting merchants raise prices if they think customers will be willing to pay more isn't a concession to greed. Rather, it creates much-needed incentives for people to think harder about what they really need and appropriately rewards vendors who manage their inventories well.[14]

Superstorm Sandy is an extreme example, but whenever and wherever a natural disaster hits the allowance of free-market pricing—with no restriction of Profit Motive—could help save lives.

Leading up to almost every snow storm on the East Coast, a region accustomed to mild weather patterns, there is a rush to the grocery store. However, if grocery stores were allowed to raise their prices without being accused of price gouging they might be able to avoid the last-minute rush and provide a greater incentive for households to maintain a better preparation level.

Furthermore, right before a natural disaster, people evacuate. We have all seen the long lines stretching from gas stations as people attempt to fill up on their way out of town. During the mad dash, gas stations often run out of gas because of the high demand and inability to raise prices. If they could raise their prices they wouldn't run out of gas (at least not as quickly) because the operator could match price with demand. Therefore, a bus driver that could potentially evacuate many people might find it more valuable to fill up his tank than a person driving alone in a car, and who might even be willing to pay to ride on the bus. This price difference alone could lead to less vehicles on the roads and a more efficient and effective evacuation.

Evacuation is important, but the recovery is also often overlooked. Because many suppliers can't change prices for fear of being accused of price gouging, many resources are distributed ineffectively. The person repairing a doghouse is able to compete for building supplies with someone who is building a shelter for hundreds of people. It would not take much of a price increase to convince the doghouse owner to delay construction, and the shelter builder would be happy to have access to the supplies as well as the people who could potentially stay there.

Price gouging is really just a price movement to an extreme equilibrium point. By restricting the movement, the market inefficiencies cause dramatic, scary, and possibly fatal outcomes.

In the end, prices are not always set at the equilibrium point if a company wants to maximize profit. The equilibrium point is where a price would be set in a market that has stabilized and has no outside interference. Imperfect knowledge, competition gaming, regulations, and taxes all play a role in obscuring what prices should be and force and/or allow businesses to make decisions that deviate from that point. Good companies, or Bob the barber, take advantage of these glitches in market pricing.

If pricing motive, which is where the Profit Motive rubber hits the road, is sufficiently understood, additional insight can then be gleaned almost every time. Is a product dramatically underpriced? Are they producing the same thing, but more efficiently? Do they have a better supplier, or do they just not know the value of their product? Is the product not priced correctly for the long run so that they need to re-price in the near future, or have they just hired an all-female staff whom they are paying 20 percent less than their competitors? Or, is the product overpriced? Is the market changing and they are overvaluing their product, or are they providing a better quality product altogether? The price that someone sets says a lot, but that "something" can be hidden behind the multiple decisions that have gone into setting the price in the first place.

Additionally, when setting prices, the decision of where to set the price vs. the equilibrium point can signal a lot of information about your brand or dramatically increase your bottom line, just like Bob the barber. Or, like Rockefeller did with oil, it can completely decimate your competition. Price is a signal; it is a weapon in the capitalist arsenal, and it is a key to realizing profit.

Employment

When an employer hires someone they are not looking to do a public service. They are looking to profit.

Therefore, if the employee costs more than what they add to production, an employer will likely not hire that person or attempt to find a method to increase that worker's production. From the minimum wage to cries of sexism, accusations against employers as well as decisions of employers can be understood and defended through the Profit-Motive lens.

A good place to start is the argument over the existence of a pay gap or the academic explanation of the pay gap if we can agree that it does exist. The Obama Administration put out a document in 2015 discussing the pay gap.[15] In it they show that the median woman working all year makes only 78 percent of what the median man makes. The report further goes on to show that there is also a real "Compensation Gap" in which female workers receive 5 percent less in total compensation than their male cohorts.

This is an outrage! How are business owners so dense that they haven't recognized that women will work for less, and that they can just hire all women? Think about the profit!

Given the White House's numbers it would be very profitable to hire an all-female workforce. In fact, according to those numbers the first company to do so would be more than 20 percent more effective in their labor costs. Their workers would be more productive per-dollar-spent, and they could actually increase their supply, lowering the price, and increasing demand for their fictional product while also undercutting all of their competitors and increasing their market share. More women could be hired and more people would profit.

If it is assumed that employers are seeking profit, then it is obvious that something is wrong in the way that we are measuring the pay gap and how we attribute this disparity. While there is undoubtedly some labor market employer discrimination against women that results in employers hiring equally qualified women for less pay than men, economic studies show that employer preferences are not the only factors that explain this 20 percent gap.

For instance, it should be considered that our culture socializes women from an early age to accept the role of caretaker for their families. This role likely changes women's "preferences" for the pay that they will accept for a given job. So in the job market women might prefer work that involves less risk-taking, a job that simply requires less overtime commitment because as mothers they have greater responsibility for caring their children, or what the pay gap numbers point toward is that they might accept a job that pays below market wages because their family is worth the sacrifice. The unemployement numbers from the 2008 recession point toward this phenomenon. As employers were letting employees go, they seemed to let go of men faster than women. In fact, at the time of peak unemployment during the recession, the unemployement rate among males was greater than 10.4 percent and the unemployment of women was 8 percent. But even more telling is that the unemployment rate of women across the economy often tracks below that of men, which is easily explained by the pay gap.[16] Of course, it can't be denied that some business owners are probably sexist (the dumb ones), but a business owner's main goal is profit. To take gender out of the equation for a simple example, consider that if business owners hate blue houses, but blue houses sell for 20 percent more and cost the same to build, they are likely to start selling blue houses. Allowing personal preference to dictate business decisions is a recipe for a decision that fails to bring profit.

In fact, profit-seeking is often one of the fastest ways to break through sexism, racism, or any "-ism." Because, at the end of the day, profit is the driving factor. The -ist that wins is capitalist.

One example of this is from one of my personal mentors: Terry Neese, the person who gave me the last bit of courage that I needed to make the leap from employee to business owner. She is one of my heroes, and the more I learn about her and hear from others about her the more I find out that I am not alone.

"I built my original business, Terry Neese Personnel, from a small startup to an full fledged business that my daughter now runs and it has now placed hundreds of thousands of people in jobs since 1975. It hasn't always been easy. At one point they closed the street that my office was on because of construction—for two years. I overcame those challenges, and entrepreneurs have always overcome those kinds of challenges—it is a part of our DNA.

However, that doesn't mean that we don't need encouragement.

Profit Motive, as you say, is a driving force for many of us in starting our own companies. We see it as a way to lift the ceiling on what we might be able to earn in our lifetimes. But I don't think that Profit Motive is enough for an entrepreneur to make the jump. They need that burning passion to lead, the yearning to change the world, or sometimes just the stubbornness to know that they can't work for someone else.

I started the PEACE THROUGH BUSINESS® Program not to teach those traits to our students from Afghanistan and Rwanda, but to unleash what I knew was already there.

Then we just let capitalism work its magic. Profit creates some pretty amazing incentives to adapt worldviews."

—Terry Neese

From an interview I held with her on January 13, 2017

After building Terry Neese Personnel into a successful business, Terry then founded Women Impacting Public Policy and built it into a powerful organization as well. Terry eventually left there to take a position with the first Bush Administration and then started a new organization: the Institute for the Economic Empowerment of Women (IEEW). One of IEEW's projects is one of the smartest and most effective ways that I have seen to effect change: It's called Peace Through Business (PTB). It doesn't address only the wage gap; Terry's program, now in its eleventh year, addresses the role of women in cultures altogether.

The Peace Through Business program teaches business to women in Afghanistan and Rwanda, and the top fifteen students of each class are given another month of classes in the United States. Graduates of the PTB program have gone on to create some very successful businesses in both Afghanistan and Rwanda. One of these, a soccer ball factory, was even one of the stops that Secretary of State Hillary Clinton made when she visited Afghanistan.

Terry's program relies on Profit Motive as the primary driver of change, and other experts in human rights issues are starting to notice the effectiveness of her program. There are several benefits that come from Terry's outreach, but the one relevant to the current conversation is that many of the graduates of the program hire both males and females.

Many of the women in both Afghanistan and Rwanda have been oppressed by the culture that they live in, but as business owners they realize that expressing or using their business as a social justice platform will likely lead to the failure of their business. On the other hand, looking at their businesses from a higher level, just the fact that these women own businesses in these regions is a big deal (and in some cases possibly illegal). More importantly, it is very hard for a male working in a women-owned business to sustain his hatred, disdain, or belief that women are less than men when a woman is responsible for writing him the paychecks that allow his family to survive.

The motivation to earn an income and support a family can help overcome sexism and even cultural norms that do not benefit women. Sexists are driven by Profit Motive like everyone else, so that when confronted with a choice between sexist behavior or making more of a profit by working with women are likely to take profit. Although, to be clear, a sexist could very easily see their profit today as providing a larger opportunity to be a sexist tomorrow. However, since being a sexist means cutting off half of the marketplace (all women) at the start, it is likely that the unrealistic and absurdist viewpoint of a sexist will change over time.

Additionally, while it is obvious that the Left uses the pay-gap data incorrectly, the overall data is apparently accurate and shows a significant disparity exists, but given our knowledge of Profit Motive, it can help us look for the reasons for this in places that make more sense—like industry and gender-based choices and disparities in education that lead women to have different experiences and values that can't be blamed on discrimination by male employers in the labor market.

Disproving the myth of the reason for the statistical pay-gap— and showing how sexism can be overcome—helps illustrate that a Profit Motive dominates business decisions and explains how entrepreneurship is driven by a this motive, there is another employment debate that helps define much of the rest: minimum wage.

Minimum wages are created by the government. I have long referred to the minimum wage as the "Death Wage" that has been codified by the Left. The public policy debate over the minimum wage routinely attempts to peg the minimum wage to the poverty rate. However, between the passage of a minimum wage bill and it's signing into law and the time when the law actually goes into effect, inflation has already caused the new federal "minimum wage" amount for a full-time job to be below the poverty line (For instance the current minimum wage of $7.25 per hour for a person working 40 hours a week yields an annual income of only $15,080, and the current poverty level for a family of two is $16,078 (see epi.org).

By itself, that distortion might be bad enough, but there is more to this because the minimum wage distorts the entire hourly wage market. Without the minimum wage, many hourly wages would likely be higher, but the codification, or government approval of a certain level that the government has deemed acceptable, maintains a downward drag on pay for low and unskilled labor. What this means is that low-skilled, low-paid employees are likely to receive less than they would if we did not have a minimum wage. The hits don't stop there though. There are plenty of jobs that business owners would fill and people whom they would hire if they didn't have to pay the minimum wage. When there is a relatively high minimum wage, many business owners might not find it profitable to hire a worker to fill a position. An example of this was recently proven by a study that followed increase of the Seattle, Washington, minimum wage from $11 to $13 an hour. The conclusion of the paper was that increasing the minimum wage "lowered low-wage employees' earnings by an average of $125 per month in 2016."[17]

These decisions distort economic growth. I despise the minimum wage, but because of the Left's persistence in wanting to increase it, the minimum wage discussion has increased productivity in recent years by providing a financial motive to accelerate automation for jobs previously held by minimum-wage employees. McDonald's has discussed using self-ordering, Panera has already installed many self-ordering point of sale machines, and the company that manages the convenience stores in the House of Representatives in Washington has done away with all employees except the occasional stocker.

Some of these decisions would have been made without the minimum wage. But most of these businesses would have probably taken longer to evolve to automated service. For instance, as demand for labor decreases it would be natural for the price of labor to decrease, but because the minimum wage fails to allow that change, employers are moving towards automation faster than they would want to without the minimum wage. As technology continues to improve, this effect will become even more pronounced.

An artificially high minimum wage also dampens economic growth. For instance, if a startup is looking to expand and can only afford a $7/hour employee, but the minimum wage is $10/hour, the startup would necessarily need to delay hiring until the owner can both afford the higher-paid employee as well as justify that level of production. In this situation more people are left jobless, fewer people gain experience, the business grows more slowly, fewer people benefit from the product, and less taxes are paid at every level. A higher minimum wage can have a dramatic effect on the economy—a bad one.

According to Iain Murray of the Competitive Enterprise Institute:

> Minimum wages benefit some workers, but come with tradeoffs that hurt others. The bleak litany of tradeoffs includes, but is not limited to: firings; hour cuts; reduced or eliminated non-wage perks such as insurance, vacation days, and complimentary parking and meals; lower annual bonuses; and reduced purchasing power due to higher prices. Moreover, some workers are never hired in the first place, and these willing workers are disproportionately young and minority. No amount of wishing can make these unintended consequences go away. Intentions are not results.[18]

Importantly in this case, a high minimum wage, a minimum wage that is above what someone would take to do a job, can ignore the Profit Motive of someone willing to work for a lower wage. Young workers are eager to gain experience, and rather than not having this opportunity, many would gladly give up the extra few dollars to gain the experience.

Minimum-wage employees are not the only ones to look at their job through a Profit Motive lens. Higher-level, better-educated, and experienced employees look at their jobs the same way. However, higher level employees often put less emphasis on direct monetary compensation and increasingly value other parts of their jobs.

In the end employers need employees, and individuals need to make money.

The Profit-Motive lens helps us to decide how their relationship is going to take shape—who will be employed by the business, how many employees and how many males and females, what they will get paid, and what their responsibility will be. These decisions aren't made to benefit the employee per se; they are made to benefit "Profit." However, if some, many, or all decisions don't benefit the employee, it's unlikely there will be successful employer-employee relationships, and the employers will be left to fend for themselves—as their business quickly fails.

Startups

"The only time that communism works is in a startup."
—Doug Humphrey, speaking at a Capitol Hill Briefing

Doug Humphrey is known as the Father of Managed Hosting and an internet pioneer. Unfortunately, I didn't have the opportunity to know Doug before his major successes (and failures), but I have had the opportunity to know him as a friend and mentor as well as swapping hundreds of hours of stories. And, judging by our time together, I don't think that he has changed too much, although if he wants to start a business today he won't have a full-time day job slowing him down.

One of my favorite lessons I learned from Doug through our hours and hours of conversation is that a startup may be one of the few places that true communism can actually exist.

Of course as a capitalist that loves entrepreneurship the story always makes me initially cringe, but given that the communism in this case (short-term pain) is being endured for the possibility of participating in an exit (long-term gain) his story is one of the more eye-opening looks into the life of a startup business as well as the Profit Motive of an entrepreneur and the first few employees.

I have had a hit a few home runs, a few doubles, and a few singles, but I have also struck out.

A lot of people will say that losses and failures are important for an entrepreneur—and I wouldn't trade mine. However, it isn't the act of failing that it is important. Failing sucks. It is what you learn from a failure. If failing makes you better, then failing is important.

The life of a successful entrepreneur is often like the businesses that they run—iterative. Wins and losses, wins and losses, and wins and losses, but the secret is to continue to build on the last loss and to keep the curve accelerating.

Investors look for this curve—it is an indicator that the entrepreneur is not just working hard, but that they can learn. They are looking to win—They are seeking profit.

Doug Humphrey

From an interview I held with him on January 16, 2017

When Doug started the company, Digex, that really put him on the map as an entrepreneur he was still working a full-time job at Tandem Computers. Digex started in his house where they wrote the code, and hosted the hardware, and at farmers markets where they signed people up one-by-one for access to the internet. Doug realized that when students at the time left college, they also largely left their access to email. That realization was the birth of Digex. Doug's "goal" didn't just easily turn into reality. It took long hours, it took debt, it took risk, and it took a bit of following his gut.

For instance, one of his first employees wasn't even old enough to drive, but he was an internet security pioneer partially because there really wasn't anybody else doing it at the time. Doug realized the young man's talent, understood that it was a key to his company's success, and did what was necessary to hire the young expert. This included Doug driving out to the young man's parent's house with his girlfriend, now his wife, to sit down and have dinner with the parents and explain the mission, vision, and technological needs of his company while also doing his best to prove that he wasn't creepy, and in fact his company and he needed their son's talent and genius.

It worked, and that summer the security expert slept on Doug's couch in the basement, so that his parents wouldn't have to drive him back and forth at the weird times of day/night that programmers tend to operate.

It seemed an exercise in "From each according to his ability, to each according to his need."

Doug didn't really pay the couch dweller. He was busy investing everything that he could into the company, but if his new young employee needed food it was in the kitchen. Similarly, if the programmer and couch dweller asked for something that he needed then he got it if the money was available. It was almost this way until Digex raised its first round of Venture Capital funding.

The early employees weren't all non-driving couch dwellers though. Some of his employees had mortgages, families, and kids. The employees still didn't get paid—well, not really paid. But Doug would walk around the office and ask what people needed.

Some of the people who lived with Doug (there were more people than the just the basement dweller) almost never asked for money, while others who had houses needed to pay electric bills. It didn't matter whether the person asking for money was junior or senior, because they were working toward building the company, were a part of the team, and they all shared communally in the assets that were available to sustain them.

This is perfect communism.

Well, not exactly, since Profit Motive is real. If Digex had intended to never pay, the employees would have eventually left. If the goal of a large exit wasn't on the horizon some might not have started. The first employees who took part in the communal building of the startup loved what they were doing —that is what drove them to be good at their craft—but they invested their time and energy into Digex because they adopted Doug's dream of changing the internet.

Once Digex finally did start scaling up and did go public, those first employees were handsomely rewarded. They had received shares of the fledgling business that had grown into a rocket ship.

The early days of Digex could have been different. Maybe Doug wouldn't have let people stay in his house or eat the food in his kitchen. He might have waited to hire people until he could pay market wages. Doug could have kept all of the ownership of the company to himself. Fortunately, he didn't. If he had, he wouldn't have raised the capital to invest in equipment, ads, and space. If he had hoarded ownership of the company, he would not have been able to get others to buy into the dream and want to take ownership of the company themselves. His growth would have been slower, and it is likely that his competition would have won.

There is a story about Digex that sums up all of the gamble and sacrifice and communal beginning of a startup. Essential to Digex at that time were the servers they hosted that kept the whole operation going for their clients. One day in their second office, above a

Chinese food place in Laurel, MD, (The Silicon Trailer Park), their air-conditioning went out. That can quickly be fatal to a server, and therefore to a company. Everyone quickly surveyed their options, and the only solution was to get a new air conditioner.

However, given the communal sharing and the sparse cash in their pockets and bank accounts, they knew they were unable to put together the money to buy one—until Doug's girlfriend suddenly pulled out an envelope containing a credit card that she had just received! They hurried to the store, put a new air conditioner on her new card that was activated just at the point of this purchase, and saved the company.

Profit motive was the foundational justification for many of the participants involvement in Digex. But, in the case of the startup, it is merely the glue that helps hold the other pieces together. There is profit in the cash that people took away from Digex, but there is also profit in the shared goal that they achieved. Talking to Doug he would say that without the intermediate goals of achieving the mission, the community, the cutting edge work, and the dream of market innovation, the cash profit at the end wouldn't be enough. So when I think of the communism of a startup, I think about both the communal sharing and that one of those people also happened to save the business with a single small purchase on a small shiny, new credit card.

Investors

Kind of like the communism of a startup, a business at the full-fledged stage of a corporation is also communal. A business is the aggregate of the individuals that make it up. When dealing with a business you are dealing with an entity that is out for its own good. A business is not an individual, but when attempting to forecast future actions or interpret past actions a business should be looked at as an individual with its own profit motive—that is, if it is run correctly.

Doug Humphrey understands this better than most when he said during his interview:

> When starting a company you are it. You are the sales guy, the coder, the dev op guy, the secretary, and the holder of the ideas guy. When you have successfully built a company you can hand the "Idea" part of the business over to the group. Then the business isn't yours—it is everyone's.

This switching of roles is bigger than just growing a company, though. This is when the company, like a baby, starts walking by itself. When a company starts walking by itself, it is also no longer beholden to the profit motive of the founder alone. For instance, if the inventor of a new type of chemical process starts a company they might have a motive to personally profit from their invention. While this is expected if thinking about profit motive, they might not have the skills to fully realize that goal. Instead of building a big successful company, they might attempt to maximize their pay when what might be best for the long-term profitability is to invest in the company.

In fact, variants of this example are frequent in business. Many founders never get to lead their businesses all the way to the end. Many more that try, shouldn't. Most of the time this happens when businesses grow and take on investors.

The "investors" here aren't the easy friends and family, who while they are out for profit are also potentially supporting a business for themselves to "profit" just from helping it to succeed. Angels, venture funds, and private equity all have one goal: profit. Their contracts lay out as much. Sometimes investors will even demand that leadership must change in order for them to invest.

One of my friends, Valerie Gaydos, runs an event called the Angel Venture Forum. Entrepreneurs apply to her program in which they pitch judges, the winners attend classes, and at the end of the process the entrepreneurs pitch investors. Many of the companies she has worked with have received funding, and during the process they frequently change who is in charge of sales and marketing, but they also often bring in professional management as well.

One company that didn't bring in a professional, and their final pitch paid the price, was formed by a guy who invented a new style of ductwork that was flexible. Most of the judges in the program felt that the invention was an excellent idea with a lot of market opportunity. The inventor of the company didn't just want to produce ductwork though; he also wanted to produce coffins— yep, coffins. So instead of having a tight pitch on the last day and focusing his presentation table on the opportunities that flexible ductwork could provide builders, he confused some investors and scared off others who were not willing to fight with the owner of a business who wasn't willing to take advice.

The defense of entrepreneurs, like the ductwork coffin guy, are that they don't believe that the investors know the idea, the company, or the mission enough to make the right decisions. This assumption is unfortunate, but the main problem is that the entrepreneur doesn't recognize the profit motive of the investors.

Investors want profit. They don't want to drive a company into the ground or watch it being driven into the ground. Profit comes before ego, and sometimes to enable an idea to fully grow and mature, it takes humility to understand that the idea needs to be owned by the business instead of by an individual. A fuller understanding of the investors and their motives can help a founder accept a lesser role in order to fuel the growth in the startup that will help it take off like a rocket.

Understanding Business Decisions

If you want to understand a business decision, attempt to figure out how that decision results in more money for the company and more profit—in other words, what the profit motive was for making that decision.

One enlightening conclusion you are likely to arrive at is that businesses aren't evil. Sometimes they are poorly run; sometimes they make a bad decision or two, but in general being "evil" doesn't return a good long-run profit. Therefore, businesses are naturally largely good. However, at the same time, businesses are largely self-serving, which means that some decisions, like attempting to limit competition, aren't necessarily as good for the overall economy as they are for the individual. Limiting competition isn't necessarily evil if the government isn't used to achieve this, but a business call to limit competition should be called into question.

Also, businesses make lots of decisions. As in the startup example, not all decisions are free market-based if looked at only in the moment, and like in the barbershop example, not all of them appear rational at a first look. However, it is clear that all decisions businesses make have at their core the motive of "Profit."

PROFIT MAN

One of the best aspects, or attributes, of Profit Man is that he is predictable. He is greedy, he is self-serving, and he is selfish. When Profit Man enters a business negotiation it is easy to understand that he isn't in the room to negotiate on your behalf. It is easy to understand that he wants the best deal that he can make. So if you are looking to make a deal with Profit Man, and you want more money than he wants to give you—and less short-run profit for him—you need to convince him why the difference is worth it to him in other ways. For instance, does less profit for Profit Man now mean more money in the future? Does more money from Profit Man at the negotiation table mean that you can buy his product instead of a competitor's product? You need to explain your offer and convince Profit Man that money he doesn't want to part with is worth the risk—and Profit Man never wants to part with money.

Profit Man is also trustworthy. Don't expect charity or altruistic actions, but understand that if Profit Man is not trustworthy it would limit his long-run profit motive. Profit Man is likely one of the most trustworthy people we deal with.

When Profit Man thinks about capitalism, cronyism, prices, employees, starting a business, or investing, he isn't thinking about the fact that he is an American or a member of a community. Profit Man is thinking about his company. Many times his decisions will take into account the community or the country, but it isn't for altruistic reasons. Profit Man thinks about things outside of his company only in as far as they help his business. That means that Profit Man might support higher taxes for better roads if he is going to use those roads to increase his profit. Profit Man might support charitable or altruistic causes, but as the head of a company the support is likely for branding that he expects to profit from.

Unlike the way that some people think of Profit Man as "bad," in reality Profit Man is almost always good. But that is because being good is in his long-run best interest. The trick is acknowledging Profit Man in order to understand his motivations—and therefore how to leverage those motivations. Dangle the right type of profit in front of Profit Man and you can get him **to do almost anything**.

3

Money and "Profit Motive" in Politics

POLITICIANS ARE OFTEN DESCRIBED AS greedy and corrupt. Polls often show a wide distrust of Congress, and presidents often carry an approval rating that is much lower than 50 percent. I have had a career that has been involved with politics at almost every level, and for years I didn't think this perception was warranted. Of course, I am also a bit of an optimist.

I started off my career on Capitol Hill working for Senator Bond, a Republican from Missouri; I then worked for the Chairman of the Senate Finance Committee, Senator Grassley from Iowa, and finished up my time working for politicians with a stint for Governor Jeb Bush of Florida.

Each office was different, but in all of my time in their offices I never saw the money or the effect of money. Now, years removed from those experiences, I can see how money and "Profit Motive" shaped what I was doing and what others in the office were doing—things I didn't understand at the time.

Profit motive dramatically shapes the landscape that politicians operate on. Money and power as the potential profits are what drive politics, both rightly and wrongly, at every single stage. We can see this in voting records, the amount of money spent on lobbying, the issues that staff work on, the experience level of staff vs. lobbyists, and the difference between the messaging of a bill and the actual legislative language. Profit motive drives everyone and everything. It can't be taken out of politics, but an understanding of the warning signs of the dangers of this and understanding the motivations and incentives that exist and that people, including you and me, can use to manipulate the system, can be very valuable.

A friend has a saying, "If you run a business and aren't involved with politics, then politics are going to be involved in your business." Her point is that "Politics" and politicians are everywhere. Politicians make decisions about a great many things—from stoplight placement on our streets to business regulations and taxes. A new stoplight in the wrong place can be devastating, so someone needs to make a careful decision about where they should go.

All of a politician's decisions are governed by or based on incentives derived from profit motive. But because "politics" is such a broad issue I am going to focus on just a few situations in which profit motive is a driver. These specific instances are just a few examples, though, since politics might be one of the main areas of our lives that is mostly controlled by profit motives.

Policy and Lobbying

There was $3.2 billion spent in 2015 on lobbying.[19] From experience and discussions with congressional staff, it is evident that most of this money is spent on defensive strategies and just attempting to stay engaged. And, when a company moves towards an offensive lobbying strategy, usually their goal is a specific regulation or provision aimed at helping their own company or hurting their competitors.[20]

However, there is another type of lobbying that can really pay off for an industry. When cronies figure out ways to drive large social programs in a defined direction they stand to make millions, and even billions, of dollars.

One recent policy issue that I'll discuss later in more detail is how the private sector benefits from the government's involvement in health care. But a policy area that isn't often discussed is how profit motive has driven the debate over Social Security.

One of the biggest ongoing fights between Republicans and Democrats is over Social Security. Social Security was passed and signed into law in 1935 and is hailed by the political left as a testament to the effectiveness of social insurance. On the other side of the aisle, the political right views Social Security as the largest Ponzi scheme in the world, since the taxes paid by current workers go out the door to the current retirees.

Like most political debates, the truth is likely somewhere in the middle, but let's look at the policy debate and the profit motives that are driving it.

Social Security has three major buckets of money: retirement/old-age, disability, and survivor benefits. To pay out to these programs Social Security is collected through what you see on your paycheck as FICA taxes (Federal Insurance Contributions Act), and those taxes either go into the Social Security Trust fund in the form of IOUs, or they go directly back out to the program's beneficiaries.

Social Security and Medicare combined accounted for 41 percent of government spending in 2015, and at the end of the year there was about $2.8 trillion in the Social Security Trust Funds. Social Security is a very big program that shapes our economy, our lives, and government spending in many ways.[21]

The problem for the program is that the Social Security Trustees forecast that more will be going out than coming in by 2019, and the Social Security Trust Funds will likely be depleted by 2034. That means that program will need to be reformed well before then if it is going to survive. Because of the big amount that goes into and out of the program, along with the promises for increased benefits in the future, reform will be much easier now rather than later. But the reform proposals have some large hurdles.

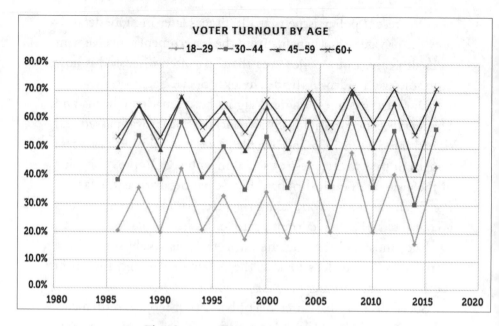

The Current Population Survey (CPS)
(Sponsored jointly by the US Census Bureau and the US Bureau of Labor Statistics)[22]

First, since it was first implemented more the three quarters of a century ago, Social Security has been a cornerstone of the Left's idea of the ability of the government to provide some level of assistance for anyone that needs it. Second, the segment of the population which receives Social Security is the one segment that votes in higher percentages than any other segment, and the second highest voting population is the segment of the population that is soon to be receiving from the program.

If forecasting the odds of reform solely using these two data points and thinking about Profit Motive, the odds of reform dramatically decrease. To reform the program, members of Congress would likely need to increase the retirement age or decrease the amount of the promised benefit. In both scenarios the voter and

Social Security recipient or soon-to-be Social Security recipient segments of the population lose out.

When looking at the odds of Social Security reform the Social Security recipients are just the beginning of the political trouble because donors also have some input. And, as people—especially the mega-wealthy—become older and their wealth increases, they are also more likely to donate to political campaigns. As we can see from the chart, there are more billionaires in the Social Security recipient stage of life than in the other stages.[23]

Furthermore, a billionaire or someone in the one percent might not necessarily need Social Security. However, taking it away from them also isn't the way to win them over and help secure their donations for the next campaign.

There are of course other reform ideas, and one of them received a lot of attention in the early 2000s: privatize Social Security.

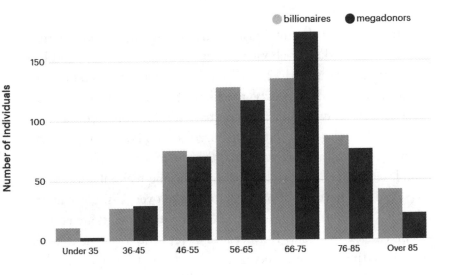

Age Distributions of Billionaires and Top 500 Donors, 2014

Privatization comes in a lot of different flavors, but in general money that is currently paid in FICA taxes goes toward benefits and the excess goes into the Social Security Fund, as discussed earlier. The money in the trust fund isn't kept in cash, but is used to pay for tanks, planes, roads, salaries, pens, hammers, etc. that the government needs to purchase. Under a privatization scheme, the money would be invested in the market instead of being spent. Under some plans the individual can choose the investments, under some schemes the investments are tied closer to the individual than others, and in different models individuals can invest in riskier portfolios. The important part of any privatization proposal is that the investment would be *invested* instead of spent.

The investment is the important part because that's where Profit Motive proves that any privatization would fail. There is just no way to correctly align the incentives of Social Security account owners who don't have much power; the very few banks that would end up making the investments, the Congress that those banks would heavily lobby, and the businesses that would eventually benefit from that cash infusion.

Investing the current Trust Funds into the market would grow the current market by about one percent. That doesn't sound like a lot, but an additional $2.8 trillion in the markets would cause a crony-driven feeding frenzy, the likes of which we've never seen. It would build cronyism into the baseline of economic forecasts because, like the ways that kings used to hand out writs of ownership to ideas and new products, the bankers could pick winners and losers that could make or break emerging technologies.

And, we have proof of this crony take over. Chile privatized their Social Security program in 1981. The investments are earning as much as 20 percent. But because of fees the investment banks charge, retirees are only seeing growth of about 5 percent in their accounts. Or more simply, retirees in Chile earn a lower percentage on their salaries invested than retirees in America.

That doesn't mean that the solution should be the government-run Ponzi scheme that we have here in the US either. The problem with the Ponzi scheme-styled Social Security system is that the Profit Motive of the bureaucrats and elected officials is to promise more today because it won't be paid for until tomorrow. And, as we proved earlier, the benefits promised today are being promised to both voters and donors, while the payment is pushed onto the people who aren't voting or donating. It is a form of political arbitrage that provides some of the worst possible "Profit Motives" in politics.

The solution is to look at "Profit Motive" and see where everything it is most aligned with the individual or retiree. There is one really effective solution, but there is second solution that is likely more politically feasible. The most effective solution is to just end Social Security altogether. It doesn't need to be stopped overnight, and given the fact that the people exiting the workforce, again who are also the voters and donors, have planned for their retirement with this program in mind. A disruptive change would be disastrous financially for many of these people and a danger politically for anyone who tried to implement it. Even for the younger people, some sort of very long off-ramp could be a useful strategy. However, the only way to really clean up the system from "Profit Motives" that all end up being detrimental to retirees is to end the program altogether.

The second solution, and probably the more feasible solution, is to turn Social Security into a retirement insurance program. Again, the basic implementation would need to be slow, but once implemented Social Security would be a program that would benefit the people who need it, and the top one percent wouldn't receive Social Security benefits like they do today. By means-testing Social Security benefits, it could truly be turned into an insurance program instead of the mandated Ponzi scheme that we are stuck with. This solution should be acceptable by both parties.

Because of the entrenched crony-lobbying campaigns on both the right and left, and the inherent political "Profit Motive" from being able to keep and spend money, it is not likely that Social Security is going to be reformed soon. But as Social Security starts costing more money than it is bringing in (estimated in 2019) the "Profit Motive" that politicians currently have goes away, and the odds of reform start dramatically increasing as the cost of the program increases and takes away money that politicians can spend on their own pet projects (thus diminishing their profit).

The Two Parties

For good or ill, we have a two-party system in the US. In large part there are differing views on the way that "Profit Motive" drives decisions that separate the two parties. While the two parties have a lot of differences, the real disagreements are often based on who you talk to. For the sake of argument here, I am going to refer to the political Left as the party of bigger government and the political Right as the party of smaller government.

The big differences between the small government Right and the big government Left is how each party has identified "Profit Motives." The big government Left is worried about the "Profit Motive" of capitalists. They, in general, don't believe that people should make a profit from health care, education, or even sometimes housing. Therefore, the big government left wants the government to take care of these "needs" since the government—surely—does not have a "Profit Motive."

The small government Right doesn't want government involved because they want profit-driven capitalists to compete for the "needs" of the people. The basic assumption is that if something is a "need" like health care the demand is there, so capitalists will compete for that business.

While I personally side with the small government right, the real issue in politics is that the current answer is some sort of a bastardized compromise system that can give rise to the worst in both conclusions.

The Left's notion of a government free of "Profit Motive" is absurd on its face. While government might not need to turn a financial profit, if voters see that an administration is throwing away their tax money, voters will want a new administration when the choice comes up. Additionally, and most importantly, each individual bureaucrat that is sitting behind a desk has their own profit motives.

Most of the bureaucrats I know want to protect their jobs and slowly move toward the top of their departments. This is the most dangerous kind, because they don't want to make a decision to spend additional money. They want to draw as little attention to themselves as possible. Going unnoticed is rewarded in the government.

Ayn Rand touched on this idea in *Atlas Shrugged*. At one point, it becomes obvious that a train shouldn't enter a dangerous tunnel because it is likely to crash. But nobody in the chain of command wants to take responsibility for making that decision, so the conductor just drives the train through the tunnel to the passengers' demise.

This doesn't just happen in works of fiction. It happens in hospitals, it happens in police stations, and it happens in our kids' classrooms. I recently spoke to a teacher who was told that she couldn't tell parents that they should seek additional services for their child. That meant that a kid in her class was less likely to get the help that he needed because she wasn't allowed to inform the parents that help was available. The dictate didn't come down because the school was scared of getting sued by parents that blame the school because their children are behind; It came down because the principal at the school didn't want to go over budget, and specialized services are expensive.

What is more expensive to society is to deal with an adult that isn't educated. However, the "Profit Motive" throughout the system isn't to make waves, but just keep moving the student through. This isn't just about money and budgets. The more students that don't make it mean worse rankings for the school, which can also dramatically hurt a career.

The "Profit Motive" of public schools is to do as much as possible with what you have, and that means that pushing or advertising the availability of costly services becomes frowned upon. We talk about this idea in the nonprofit and the health in care chapter, but identifying places like this, such as in our public school systems, where "Profit Motive" might not be leaning your direction, helps to identify places where you should be more vigilant about your own self interests.

The limited government advocates of the Right, whose notion is that capitalism will solve everything, needs a reality check as well. When programs as large Medicaid, other social welfare programs, and defense exist, the game for capitalists becomes more about the government's involvement than the market itself.

There is no issue where this is clearer than when examining the political fight over the legislation of what we call "intellectual property," referring to the creations of the mind. Intellectual property law deals with the rules that enable us to secure the legal rights to register ownership of our inventions and our literary and artistic works, and the regulation and enforcement of laws to protect our ownership of these.

One of the main tactics of a crony is to confuse politicians and staff from the supporters of small government into thinking that a bill that supports big business—their big business—is a bill that supports business in general. They, the cronies at the time, have been very effective when it comes to convincing the Right that laws about intellectual property need to be reformed.

My first experience with intellectual property legislation was with the America Invents Act, which was passed in 2012, but had been debated and deliberated for the seven years leading up to its passage. During this prolonged debate the bill got better, but the main idea of the legislation was to weaken patent rights by making them harder to enforce. It was sold by its supporters as an effort to go after the business model of the mythical "Patent Troll," a term that businesses that consider licensing patents a cost of doing business use against small inventors that sue them for patent infringement and therefore theft of their ideas, but the reality of the bill's language was much different. It makes sense that supporters of a bill would want to promote a bill in the best light possible, but if the bill wasn't about attacking Patent Trolls what was the "Profit Motive" behind the bill?

It turns out that the main supporters of the bill all view intellectual property as a cost. For instance, Google, which is largely an advertising and data company, was supporting the bill and supporting other groups that opposed the bill as well. For the main supporters, technology was a way of delivering ads and tracking data. I support this since I use a lot of technology services because they do a good job of getting me what I want, er, *need*—but this also means that technology is a cost to them. These technology companies are making money from delivering ads to me and gathering data on my online habits, and I profit from having relevant information at my fingertips more quickly and more frequently than other services have accomplished.

Like any good business, it is a symbiotic relationship. But the Profit Motive of a business is to make money. These technology companies might be able to charge their advertisers more, or they might be able to charge their users more, but then they are likely to lose at least some of their business. A third way to profit is if they can somehow decrease their costs. Then they can increase their bottom line. This is like a homebuilder trying to decrease the cost of wood. There are some ways for a business to lower these prices in a normal market, like buying in bulk, but some companies look toward government to do this for them. It is a result of cronyism, and because both sides of the deal get what they want, and since politicians make money and businesses profit, cronyism isn't something anyone on Capitol Hill is good at stopping. And we can see this is largely because there is almost no motivation to stop it.

I have never seen the effects of cronyism on Capitol Hill more striking than when dealing with Intellectual Property. In fact, I was approached several years ago and offered money just to be quiet on the issue. I was aghast, but I was also proud that my voice had been loud enough to elicit what was effectively a bribe from the other side of the debate. These kinds of conversations are fabled to happen all of the time, but in my career this was the first time I had experienced it, and I haven't had an offer like this since.

What does the fact that I received this offer mean when inspected under the prism of "Profit Motive"? It shows a lot. It proves that the supporters of the legislation have a lot to gain. It proves that my organization's argument was getting in their way. It also indicates that there is likely quite a bit of money changing hands, and that money is helping drive the issue.

The last vote by the Senate on the American Invents Act was 89-9. That is the type of vote total or percentage that just isn't seen in Congress. It is usually a huge effort to just get 60 votes in order to avoid a filibuster, and even the Patriot Act (the response bill to the 9/11 terrorist attack) got only a few more votes at 98–1. The only way to explain the votes at this level is the large amount of money that poured into the issue.

The supporters of the bill effectively leveraged the "Profit Motives" that drive Washington, DC. Now, years after the first bill passed, even more money is flowing to politicians. Many staffers who worked for the committees that passed the bills are now working for many times their earlier salaries for the companies that supported the bills, and even more bills designed to capitalize on those same profit centers are being introduced every week.

Outside of politics, the real problem with the proposed, and the already passed, intellectual property bills is that they remove the Profit Motive from the innovators. Inventors don't invent just to make other people rich. They have their own Profit Motive, and if legislation decreases that motivation, there will be effects on the rest of the economy. However, small inventors are a disperse group of people that don't have their own voice on Capitol Hill. Groups have tried to keep these diverse groups together, but this is difficult when the supporters on the other side are large, vertically integrated corporations that can afford a team of people to deliver their views, their wish list, and large checks to Congress. This has an effect on the conversation.

It is unfortunate, but Profit Motive is present in politics, and in the current atmosphere Profit Motive might be considered one of the primary drivers of public policy.

Fund-Raising

Every two years the American politics industry fills the airwaves with the most virulent, scurrilous, wall-to-wall character assassination of nearly every political practitioner in the country—and then declares itself puzzled that America has lost trust in its politicians.

—Charles Krauthammer

While there are multiple motivations for every politician's actions, one constant motivation is the need to be reelected. This is even more important than legislating because legislation can only be passed by someone who's in office. This simple fact, the incentive of politicians to be elected again, is what explains the "wall-to-wall character assassination" that Charles Krauthammer correctly identifies to describe our current political landscape.[24]

There is no place that Profit Motive in politics, or almost anywhere else in life, is more explicit than in political fundraising. Without money winning a campaign is nearly impossible, and without winning a campaign there is no chance of writing policy. The secret to getting elected with or without money is often having a big enough soapbox to deliver and advertise your message, whether that message is negative or positive. And, while some people have a large enough public profile that they are given a soapbox, for most people fundraising is the key to buying, renting, and leasing the campaign tools needed to effectively get out a message.

Members of Congress are often primarily focused on fundraising, and the members of Congress who are not will not often be in position of leadership and are also likely to be shown the door.

Fundraising happens everywhere and all the time in Washington, DC.

The heavy focus on fundraising has a major effect on the city. Every law firm has their own Political Action Committee (PAC). Lobbyists are paid a premium so that they can afford donations, and clubs all over town have lots of private rooms that can be used for fundraisers. Catering is often focused on finger foods to avoid some lobbying laws about paying for others' "meals," which otherwise could be considered buying someone's vote, the Republican clubs and the Democrat clubs are within a short walk from the congressional offices, and associations have learned to move in packs to maximize their donation impact. Meetings often occur because of a donation or possible donation, and on the Hill leadership positions are often meted out based on fund-raising. And, because raising money is so important, a full market has been built around it, including direct mail companies, list companies, event planners, and of course traditional fundraisers. And the "Profit Motive" of each of these groups is important in how it shapes Washington, DC.

For instance, the direct-mail industry is entrenched here. Companies dealing in direct mail love politicians because politicians need to get their message out, and politicians are always interested in raising money. And those two things make the direct mail companies giddy with visions of dollar signs in their head. The way that direct mail works is that a politician usually pays to rent a list. The direct-mail company makes money on that rental. Then the politician sends something out to that list. The direct-mail company usually makes money from the printing and sending of the mail as well. Then when the money comes in the company charges for handling that, too. At the end of the day, only a small portion of what the politicians raise goes back to the politician, and the direct-mail company hasn't risked any capital to provide the service. The politician doesn't really care about the percentage of return as long as the net number is big enough to help fund another round of mail and a portion of their campaign.

In any other industry the calculation on "profit" would be much different. Politicians would care more about the amount of investment that they put in and the value they get out, but money for direct mail comes from donations, and the businesses of campaigns are designed to go broke at the end. This has allowed direct mail to build a market that shouldn't really exist. Direct mail has been arbitraging the political fundraising system in Washington, DC, for years.

Interestingly, as we have moved towards computers and email, making direct mail less and less effective, the Direct Mail mafia has less of a hold on DC. However, since their return rates have not yet reached "0 percent" they are still here, although most of them are no longer wearing Guccis and Rolexes.

Diminished returns on direct mail have had other effects on fund-raising too. Now, big dollar donors are more valuable, which means that the "Profit Motive" of politicians is more focused on this group, and this means that even more power is focused on an even smaller and more powerful group of donors now.

Sometimes it isn't about power, though. It should be pretty obvious by now that people don't just hand over money because it is fun to hand over money. This is true whether they are in a store buying something, investing in a stock, or giving it as a political donation. Some people give because they believe in a given politician's leadership and therefore want them to be elected—the election is their profit. Others give because they want to steer policy. The policy is their profit. Others donate to politicians because they want power—and power is the profit. And, others give just to be in the room with other donors. For them the network is the profit.

Looking at data from OpenSecrets.com, only 46 percent of the US population gives over $200 to political candidates. Rubbing elbows with this active group of people can be valuable, and when the price of admission is only $200 that can make for a good networking investment. In fact, I believe that it was this group of donors that led my first business idea to fail.

My assumption when I started my business was that $200-donors were engaged and attempting to buy access and influence, but over the course of a campaign that raises $1 million or more, their $200 dollar donation looks more and more like a bookkeeping error. My business plan was to aggregate a few hundred of these donors and take their stories up to Capitol Hill as my full-time job. Their $200 would now be buying a full-time influencer on Capitol Hill instead of a few bumper stickers.

However, instead of an initial membership/client push that I forecast would bring in 150 members, my initial push only brought in five paying-members. I had made a major miscalculation, and I was hemorrhaging money because of it. The problem for me was that for their $200 political donation the person, or small business owner, got to spend a night with other like-minded individuals from their community and stand in solidarity with them politically for a few hours. They were doing more networking than they were buying influence. I was attempting to provide my intended clients with "profit" that they didn't want and had not been seeking. Therefore, they had no motive to stop donating to politicians and instead give my company their money.

Fortunately, I figured this out before I ran out of money, and I started working for nonprofits that were providing their donors with a benefit, and my services became one of those benefits.

I had made an error in identifying the profit motive of my target market. Like my error, in 2012 it was likely the Republican party's inability to identify the "Profit Motive" of a nonprofit that cost the Republicans the election.

Karl Rove went from the inside of the Bush Administration, where he was known as the architect, to the head of a nonprofit political organization on the outside. A move from the inside of the party to the outside of the party is a big shift, and it meant that Rove's "Profit Motive" changed and almost nobody noticed. Interestingly, Karl Rove might not have even known, or understood, that he was playing on a different team until the night of the election.

The night of the 2012 election Karl Rove had what many call a "meltdown" on live TV when Fox News called Ohio for Barack Obama. Everything that Rove knew was centered on his belief that Romney was going to win. He had ignored Nate Silver's projections on fivethirtyeight.com. He had ignored all the polling data that was being produced because he had been so certain of his selling. Karl Rove had raised and spent hundreds of millions of dollars, and paid himself a tidy sum, all while claiming that he was going to get Romney elected.

As an insider and leader in the George W. Bush Administration, Rove did the math and developed the strategy. Karl profited only by an electoral win. Once out of the Administration his job was thought of the same way—do the math and develop the strategy. But he had added more motivations to his portfolio, including the fact that he had founded not only one, but two organizations which nobody noticed.

When you are raising funds, you are selling, and without funding you can't do anything. The motivation to raise funding is a primary driver that shapes all nonprofits. Therefore, Karl Rove was selling for the livelihood of his business, reputation, brand, and ego. Karl had a lot on the line.

That all hit Karl Rove head-on when Fox News called the election. He hadn't done the math right. He knew that his world was about ready to change—fund-raising was going to become much harder for him because the donors who give large amounts didn't accrue the large amounts of money they have by being as careless as Rove has just proven to be.

To be clear, if I were running a campaign, I would still hire Rove to run it or suggest that anyone else should hire him as well. He understands strategy, and he understands numbers and voters. What Rove didn't understand is what the motivation of profit does to the way that even he processed numbers and spin. Unfortunately, for many donors, the media following Rove's previously prescient forecasts, and also it seems Governor Romney and his campaign, as well, didn't pick up Rove's change in perspective, either.

The Roles of Congressional Staff

Congressional staff have their own set of incentives, motivations, and even culture that largely dominates how they perform their job. I started my career as a staffer.

The day that I handed in my last paper in college, I returned home, finished packing, and started the drive out to Washington, DC, on a gas card and a dream. Fortunately for me, I had family that allowed me stay with them while a found a job, and then for another two years, while I got used to the city's culture and saved some money.

"Yes, being cognizant of others' motivations helps provides an effective outlook. Everyone has their own interests.

Some are based on ideological views. Others are based on business model or industry impact. And some are here to help others navigate the process. But we all have goals, including congressional members and staffers. All impact the way policy is drafted and advances or is halted.

There is no standard formula for how to weigh the impact of each. Motivations of others and one's own priorities can cause legislation to fluctuate throughout the legislative process. Just how much depends on the amount of consensus and members' comfort level with differences of opinions during their pursuit. It is those differences that impacts legislation the most. Depending on how important the effort is to a Member of Congress or an outside entity is where lines are drawn based on level of support or opposition. Those lines can adversely impact even longstanding relationships amongst stakeholders. Forecasting it is key to policymaking."

— Anonymous Capitol Hill Staffer

From an interview I held with a staffer on October 16, 2016

One of the first things that becomes clear about politics and being a Congressional staffer is that financial profit is not the driver, at least in the short run, of most of the people that sit behind any desk on Capitol Hill. They aren't paid well; they work long hours, and cost of living is high.

These factors largely drive the fact that the average age of a Capitol Hill staffer is about twenty-eight. They don't own a house, and they are probably working at their first job. On the other hand most staffers are driven, smart, and leaders, and are in politics because they want to make a positive difference.

The differences in ideologies can get in the way of staff on the political right and the political left, but the staff on both sides of the aisle are for the most part the same type of people.

I personally wanted to work on Capitol Hill because I was fascinated by the law and, therefore, the idea that laws were written by people. One of my friends says it a bit differently, but I agree: "I was drawn to the Hill initially by my interest in policy and politics. Once I experienced the issues and the process of policymaking in setting an agenda, I was hooked." Power and influence is an amazing and valuable "profit" that is addictive.

On my first day as an intern I was asked to write a speech for the Senator about the 50th anniversary of a bank. This was the first thing I had ever written for someone besides a teacher. It wasn't a task that was going to affect my kids, and it wasn't a task that was going to affect the overall economy, but it was something that the founders of the bank would see and they had worked fifty years to celebrate that day. The next day when I went down to record the video with the Senator, I heard him read the words based on my research and that were likely going to be heard by everyone that worked at, for, and with that bank. It was at that moment that I was hooked. Even on my first day, I had done something significant.

The "power" involved with writing that simple speech might sound small, but consider that almost all of the speeches that our elected officials are giving are written by staffers that often don't have much more experience than what I had on my first day.

Profit Motive doesn't just drive the staff, Congressional staff also meet with people every day who have their own motivations. Lobbyists, advocates, and district residents make their way into Congressional offices to express their own concerns as well as the concerns of their clients. These meetings happen all the time, and while the staff are often prepared to filter the messages that the visitors deliver, they are also subjected to them frequently enough that eventually messages can start driving changes in the way that a staffer thinks, writes, and works on any given issue.

Staffers understand this too. When talking to one of them recently, he said:

Those who come to a congressional office to meet about policy all have a goal. Sometimes it is a specific request about potential legislation or regulation at an agency. Other times it is to educate an office about their industry or organization. But savvy stakeholders see value in building a relationship with an office because you never know when they might be on the agenda and want to provide some input. Finding areas of common ground furthers the discussion—even during times when their views run counter to a national legislative push.

It is the long-term relationship that runs Washington, DC, and a lot of why people that have been here for an extended time tend to act in a way that those on the outside would call "establishment." Long-run relationships are hard to create and maintain, so when you have one, the "Profit Motive" is to keep them. These long-run relationships help explain the norms and hard to change nature of Washington, DC.

There are of course positives to these relationships and also negatives. Fortunately, the "Profit Motive" of the individual is likely more tied to their job than their relationship, so things don't often go off the rails, but sometimes even that assumption breaks down. Staff, that I am not going to call out here, often write and pass bills before going to work for the companies that just benefited from their work.

It doesn't stop during the 9-to-5 portion of Capitol Hill staffers' day (and their days aren't really 9-to-5 either). "Profit Motive" also drives the after-hours scene in Washington, DC, and unfortunately for new staffers it isn't in the free-flowing alcohol direction of the past. The private lives of staffers is affected for several reasons, including legal and profit-driven reasons.

When I started on Capitol Hill, lobbyists could still buy drinks for basically everyone at almost any time. So a normal night was that of a lobbyist opening a bar tab for a few offices, basically anyone in the bar, and offices on Capitol Hill coordinating where they were going to drink—for free—on a given night. There has been a lot of alcohol that has been served on Capitol Hill through the years. These parties were usually bi-partisan because it made sense for the lobbyist to bring as many people together as possible so they could potentially build an even bigger network.

However, in 2007 a new lobbying bill was passed that made it almost impossible to open up bar tabs anymore. That means that staffers no longer have the incentive to co-mingle with their peers on the other side of the political aisle. First, they have limited resources, so why spend it with someone that you are likely to argue with for a large portion of the night. Second, as a young staffer hanging out with the other side of the aisle isn't going to help you career on Capitol Hill, which is based on moving up within your own "gang" or your side of the political aisle.

Staffers are making rational decisions based on their own "Profit Motives," but they now have fewer connections with staffers on the others side of the aisle, and this has a long-run effect on the legislative process.

Of course this is just one of the ways that Profit Motive affects politics, but when the "Profit Motive" of the staffers who run Capitol Hill is to *not* become friends with the people they need to work with, less gets accomplished. This lobbying provision was well-intentioned, but has done more harm than good by incorrectly playing into staffers' Profit Motive. The system is already in major need of help.

Politicians and Profit Motives

Fortunately or unfortunately, most politicians, at least on the federal level, aren't in their jobs for the money. They definitely make a respectable amount of money while in federal office, but many of them were making more on the outside or expecting to make more on the outside once they retire—or are retired from elected office. That means that they are in the job for a profit other than money, and since politics is competitive it makes sense that for a lot of them that "profit" is winning. The drive to win is something that I see in a lot of politicians. Some are better at it and others less so, but most politicians, like athletes, are driven toward winning. Winning is their "Profit Motive."

I have had the to opportunity to be close with several politicians and lots of staffers over the course of my career. One of the politicians that I have had the privilege of spending a fair amount of time with is the Chairman of the House Rules Committee Pete Sessions. Despite his busy schedule, he let me sit down with him to interview him about the idea of Profit Motive in his world of politics.

I ended my conversation with Chairman Sessions by asking him about his personal Profit Motive. I wanted to know what drove him, and his answer was powerful enough that I want to start off with it here:

> Winning. I don't do this for myself. I have missed lots of personal opportunities since I have been in Congress that would have been valuable personally, but the country has benefited from my sacrifices—at least I think that I can prove that. Since I have been here, I have helped keep us from bankrupting the country even though we are definitely in bankruptcy. We should be spending $1 trillion more a year, and we would under average circumstances. But the Republicans held spending in 2011, 12, 13, 14, 15, 16, and now 17, flat. And, I don't believe you get back by slashing and burning. I have never been driven by slashing and burning. I am a revenue guy. I played quarterback; I am for offense. But if the president won't give us offense, or what we want, we are going to hold . . . Look, we have taken away a lot of things, but by and large we are at 2008 spending levels.

Sometimes a short quote doesn't quite do the conversation justice, but the answer from the chairman is one of the reasons that he is a leader. It reminded me of the same emotional lift that I got from half-time speeches in the football locker room—although it lacked the thrown marker, water bottle throw, or crass language that can go along with those speeches. The chairman's eyes were brighter when he said them, and he even sat up straighter in his chair. He meant it. He does his job in order to win and make the country a better place because of it. The rest of the conversation that the chairman and I had came into focus after his inspirational monologue. He had been laying out the tools that he personally used to win: the tools that he used to "profit."

Chairman Sessions represents Texas's 32nd district, and he has been in Congress since 1997. He is a known leader among the Republicans, and in his role as Chairman of the Rules Committee is one of the single most powerful Congress members. What I like and admire most about Chairman Sessions, though, is the way that he runs his office. I have attempted to explain it several ways to people who haven't experienced his office, but the best way to explain it is by visiting the Apple Store. It is active, it is open, and it is effective in promoting its product:

Pete Sessions explains his methods:

"Here's an example. I had a member that was of limited ability and had limited time, but they wanted to be seen as a winner to make their goal. He said, 'I can't raise money in Nebraska.'

I said, 'I'll tell you what. I have a plan for you.'

He said, 'you do?'

I said, 'yes.'

I picked five rich areas that are held by Democrats that no Republican goes in and I introduced him and told him,

'Go to the newspaper, go to talk radio, go to the Republican clubs, here is the donor community. I'll come in and help you, but you go and work those leads.'

The member did his homework and worked Boston, Massachusetts when nobody had. I helped him and he made his goal. That member still has friends in Boston . . ."

—Chairman Pete Sessions on "Teaching Others to Win"

From an interview I held with the chairman on October 16, 2016

When you enter the chairman's main office, two or more people are there to greet you. They might take your coat or they might get you a Dr. Pepper; they will often offer visitors cake or something else to eat if that is available somewhere in the office. Then visitors will often notice that the door to the chairman's office is open, and you can usually hear his assuring voice, or his kind voice, or his booming, excited voice coming out. If he is pacing around the office signing photos, organizing papers, or lining up with someone else to take a picture and sees you out on the couch waiting to come in to see him—or just sitting there at all—he will invite you in take a picture with you and often sit you down to participate in whatever meeting he is having at the time. In fact, when I sat down with him to talk specifically about this book, at various times in the interview a constituent came in for a picture, staff came in and sat down, and people from two different meetings scheduled after me were in the room listening—and even participating in the interview.

He has a fun office, and the important thing for me is that the office has this feeling purposely. Pete considers himself the product and his constituents the customers. His understanding of the voter/elected official relationship is a perfect "Profit Motive." The constituents of Texas' 32nd district voted for him, their taxes pay for him, his staff, and their offices, and they want to see a profit from their vote. Chairman Sessions wants to deliver them that profit, because that helps him get re-elected and eventually fulfill his own goals or reach his personal profit.

When talking about the data collection, which is a big deal in his office, Chairman Sessions grabbed a packet of papers from his desk. The stapled packet had several pages and on each page was a picture of one of the chairman's staff members with Pete, and below that were their issues, their email, and their phone number. In our interview he lit up while looking at the document and said:

> I actually put their personal phone numbers on there and no staff likes that. I want people to know that we are accountable to them, that we aren't going to hide. We aren't going to say one thing and do something different. We are going to address people. We are going to be respectful, and we are going to allow people to make mistakes without calling them stupid because they are the customer. It's my fault that they didn't really understand where I was or what I was doing, but I am asking them to understand that I would like to explain myself, and the vast majority of people get that.

It doesn't just stop with giving out his staff's emails though. The chairman is big on data collection and usage. He has his staff collect business cards from everyone that comes into the office, and the pictures he insists on taking aren't just used as souvenirs for his guests. They are accustomed to making the visitors feel at home the next time they visit the office because his front desk staff will upload them to his digital picture frame. Additionally, at every meeting that he or his staff have with a visitor they make sure to upload the notes to their data system, and, most importantly, they check them before the next meeting with that person.

This drive for information is at least partially born out of Pete's background—he was a salesman. Not only was Chairman Sessions a salesman, but in his time at Southwestern Bell Telephone

Company his district in Dallas was the #1 district in the country for 39 straight months. He won then and he is still winning. And, one of the interesting points that he made is that his leadership during his time at Southwestern Bell wasn't magic. His leadership was about showing that he cared about the employees. The weekend before he was even scheduled to start he came in and cleaned the place from floor to ceiling himself. Once he started he immediately organized the mail, he ordered a new ice machine, he implemented casual Friday, and he made sure to engage his employees.

As a manager Pete understood that his employees were what was going to make him successful. That is same lesson that he tries to teach people interested in running for Congress today. When talking about his time at the National Republican Campaign Committee where he led the Republicans to their current majority by winning a net gain of 63 seats and ushering in 89 new Freshman, he said:

> "Walk doors," I told everyone of our people. If you want to run for Congress you better walk 500 doors, because when people answer the door they are going to say, "Why are you running?" You get it down after 500. You do not have it down before your 500th.
> It is hard . . . You go to enough doors you will have down why you are running. If it is just against something rather than what you are for, you are not going to win. You have to actually be for something.

Door-walking is important, understanding your constituents is important, but what the chairman was suggesting is that what these aspiring politicians do is to figure out their Profit Motive. It takes a potential profit to both fully motivate the politician, but without a true Profit Motive to show the voters, they won't trust the candidate, share in the goal, or share in the profit when the goal is reached.

This idea of needing a goal—a potential profit—isn't just a talking point for Chairman Sessions though. He also took this lesson to the NRCC when he took it over and created the organization that was ready to win a majority.

> Essentially . . . we were dealing with an organization that was not focused. They didn't know what they were doing. They were replaced, and it was a political arm of leadership rather than designed to win. I served as a vice chairman of the committee for twelve years. During those twelve years, literally, I was never asked to do anything. Nobody was in charge. You just could not get people to respond back to you. You were a nothing, even as a member of Congress. It was a completely a staff-driven operation. So, what I did is that I came in and defined what we were going to do. The first thing is a goal; we never had a goal.

The chairman didn't stop there; at the annual fundraising gala, the chairman sat at table 218. That was the number of seats that Republicans needed to win. He was setting goals and giving them the plan to get there. With winning as his motivation, the chairman was doing everything that he could to accomplish that, and other people picked up on his goal. They fed off his drive and it worked. Even today, the chairman thinks that if more people had bought into his goals, the Republicans could have won another ten seats in 2010.

In the end, winning more means that Chairman Session is likely to do better when he leaves public office. However, he is so good at winning that he might just stay and continue his personal, not monetary, profit from the "win." And, admittedly, in a chapter about money and politics, it is kind of ironic to discuss the outlook of a politician who is more concerned about winning than fund-raising. But, as discussed earlier, one of the chairman's talents was his ability to raise funds and to bring in money in a way that nobody else does. The chairman profited then by helping people, and he worked hard enough and won enough seats for the party that a lot of people owe him favors. In politics that short of debt often equals money.

Bringing It All Together

I have demonstrated how Profit Motives exist in politics just as they do in our business lives and our personal lives. We are driven by financial goals and a desire for power to win and move our country in a direction that is good for us.

When a company decides to hire a lobbyist, the members have made the calculation that their investment is going to pay off more than it cost them. How the lobbyist provides that value varies, but at the very least it involves attempting to change legislation in a way that benefits their company.

Congressional staff understand the basic motivations of the lobbyists, but the fact is that the lobbyist is usually paid more the three times what the staffer is being paid and often much, much, more. Everyone understands the game, and the large corporation wants to hire the best player. That means they are willing to find and pay the best player.

That also means that the lobbyist often has more experience, institutional knowledge, and even more intelligence about the company's issues than the staffer he is dealing with. While the Congressional staffer has political power—the power of advising his boss how to vote, the power to inform other staff and members about a lobbyists agenda, an even the right to refuse the meeting altogether—the lobbyist still has one more tool at his disposal.

Money is everywhere in politics, and this is the lobbyist's best tool. But, while there is a lot of money involved in politics, the rules about money mean that bribery isn't an option on the table— well at least not for the people willing to follow the laws. The primary use of money is having direct access to the elected officials. Access to elected politicians means that you might be able to directly convince them of the need to act on an issue, and if they agree the staff can be bypassed and can just be tasked by the congressman or congresswoman to help the work of the lobbyist.

To complicate matters, lobbyists can't just be banned. In addition to their First Amendment freedoms, congressional staffers usually need these experts to draft legislation on the complicated matters in their portfolios. (I have never met a staffer that knows how to run a doctor's office, hospital, or insurance company.) While the experts that the staff talk to while working on legislation in these areas deliver stilted information, if the staff were to work without this information the legislation would turn out a lot worse. Furthermore, the staff often want to work with as many lobbyists as possible because of their own Profit Motives.

Most staffers are only on Capitol Hill for a few years. If someone has worked on Capitol Hill for five years they are considered tenured (not an official title), and it is rare that someone makes it to ten years. The good employees usually move on and take one of the high-paying lobbying jobs to put their hard won knowledge to work.

The way to leverage Profit Motive in politics, and what I do, is not to attempt to outbid anyone in the money game—that is a fool's errand. The best way to leverage the motivations of alphas, which is a good way to describe both congressional staff and elected officials, is to be a trusted source of information for them. I explain it to people as avoiding the marble-lined lobby and instead pulling up to the loading dock where the real work takes place. I've already covered the fact that staff are overworked and underpaid. Offering to help with their work can go a long way. They say that information is power, but in this situation the value of information still plays second fiddle to cash.

Following Profit Motives in politics can be confusing and difficult because they are everywhere, and they all make a significant difference in the direction of policy debates. But awareness of them is a good start.

Profit Man

Profit Man doesn't just have one suit. He doesn't just run companies and roll in a pile of money. Profit Man is everywhere, and one of his favorite places to be is on top of a soap box with others listening to him talk. It is a different type of profit, but leadership, competition, and ego are a part of every politician's profit motive and they give Profit Man what he needs to survive.

There are, of course, also money profit motives that are all around and temping to the political Profit Man. While they are rarely in the form of envelopes filled with actual cash, they are delivered to politicians in the form of promised jobs, jobs for family members, staffers, campaign contributions, or more jobs in their home state.

Most of the time the political Profit Man just sits back and takes it all in. He taxes people and then hands out the money as he sees fit, which allows him to extract as much profit as he can from others people's money.

One way to restrict both the urge of Profit Man to become a politician and restrict the ability of Profit Man to profit from being a politician is to limit the size of government. Identifying Profit Man as a politician becomes harder and harder as government grows. When Profit Man only has a limited set of decisions to make each and every day, there is a limited amount of profit he can reap from his constituents. If the political Profit Man is confronted with an unlimited amount of choices, decisions, and public policies, there is an almost boundless amount of profit that he can reap and destruction that he can cause. The nature of taxation is that small bits of money are taken from a lot of people. So, Profit Man only needs to provide a small benefit to everyone to fulfill their profit motive and make them happy.

4

Media

As I was sitting in front of a TV camera for a live interview for the first time, I was slightly sweating under the glare of the studio lights and running through my talking points in my head. I had no idea what was about to happen. I just knew they wanted me to be good and that achieving this was likely to require some help.

The studio that I was sitting in was the first DC studio for One America News, and at that time it was a startup cable news channel with the goal of competing to the right of Fox News. I had initially been contacted as a backup for someone, but after talking to the show's host, Graham Ledger, they decided that they wanted me on the show weekly. It is likely that the show just needed people, but I was flattered. At that point in my career, I knew that "no" wasn't the right answer.

The day before the first interview I received the topic that we would be discussing, and I was asked to send talking points. I didn't even know that I would be tipped off to the topic beforehand, but I was pleasantly surprised. I did my research, put together the talking points, and sent them to the show's producer. The day of the show, I decided to take public transportation to the studio, which to most places in Washington, DC, wouldn't have been a problem, but the studio was in the basement of the *Washington Times* which isn't in downtown DC and is 1.5 miles from even the closest bus stop. I eventually got off the bus that I was on and hailed a cab, but not before I had fully sweated through my shirt and was losing the extra time I'd allowed myself. I ended up arriving at the studio early enough that my shirt dried out, but my mind was still racing from the anxiety of being late when I sat down in the studio.

The headquarters of One America News is in California, so it was just me, myself, and I behind the desk in the studio. I sat in the chair as the cameraman/studio manager put the earpiece in my ear and mic onto my jacket before leaving the room. After he left it was just me with a camera pointed in my direction in a dark room with the bright video lights pointed in my direction. The camera was almost hard to see, but its lens was black and kind of bare. I stared at it, and started reviewing my talking points.

Once the host's voice came over the earpiece, it was game time. He gave his intro, played a little video (that I couldn't see), and then introduced me while asking the first question. The whole event was a blur, but it went well and accounted for about eight minutes of his hour show.

Talking Heads and Radio Guests

I have now done that same setup maybe a hundred times, and while I am used to looking at the blank lens and imagining the person who I am talking to on the other end, the biggest lesson that I learned is that it is in the show's interest for me to look good. I shouldn't have been nervous. If the host asked me something that I didn't know about, yes, I would look dumb or ill-informed, but the show would have lost credibility. The show's motivation was for me to look good, because that reflects positively on them, which is good for their profit.

The channel itself, One America News—like any business— seeks financial profit. Their profit comes from several sources, but essentially it all comes down to whether the shows on the channel are worth watching. The "Profit Motive" of a political show, even a partisan one, is to be both entertaining and credible. If the show loses credibility, viewers are less likely to come back. In fact, even when a show has someone on who doesn't agree with them, they need to be credible. The first time that I met Graham Ledger in person he explained the relationship between show hosts, producers, and guests in a very concise way that I still think about today. He said, "The producer's job is to make me look good, and my job is to make you look good."

I continued to do the Daily Ledger for more than a year, and Graham still has me on occasionally to go over numbers, like polls or budgets. As the channel grew in viewership and the show grew in popularity, the value/profit that I provided Graham decreased. Conversely, as I learned how to do these news spots competently, *my* profit from doing the weekly spot diminished. So now Graham and I both focus on setting up slots we can both hit out of the park together and provide the best value for both of us. That helps his show continue to grow and lets me make a bigger impact and be a better guest by focusing only on issues where I'm an expert.

It is hard to convince a channel like CNN or FOX News to give a person their first interview, like my time on One America News was for me, and it is hard for a new channel like One America News to secure interviews with experienced media personalities. The profit that we each secured from our early relationship was valuable, and our profit was mutual although our motivations were different. This is the way that guest spots work. Each side has their own profit motive, and each side wins.

One of the big things to understand when watching TV, whether it is your favorite morning show or a cable news show, is that guests aren't paid to be on the show. As discussed, guests are on these shows for their own benefit, which means that the relationship is symbiotic. On the rare occasion that a guest is paid to make an appearance on a show, the person is still only paid a fractional part of their market value.

This wasn't always the case. But as the 24-hour news cycle has developed, and the competition to be a guest on the shows started to increase, the people who run the channels realized that they no longer have to pay for quality personalities. Now people appear on television for their own profit motive.

The most common arrangement for a talking head, like me, is to hire a public relations expert to make introductions and secure interviews. (Basically like having an agent in Hollywood.) This arrangement is common because it is the best way to address the profit motives of both the guest and the show. Guests want to be on shows and shows want quality people.

It's likely that the expert has relationships with producers and hosts on shows at every level and on many different stations. Since the experts' goal is to get their clients on these shows, they need to make sure that they maintain these relationships. If the expert attempts to place a person who isn't good, for whatever reason, the producer will be less likely to listen to the expert next time. Therefore the producer can be reasonably assured that the talking head of the day will be a quality guest. For the person trying to get on a show, the fact that the communication expert has maintained these relationships means that their odds of going on air are greater than someone who just emails the producer out of the blue.

I have used experts to place articles for me, get radio slots for me, and get me onto TV. I like developing my own relationships, but these professionals can be very helpful because most producers and hosts are very cautious about who they have on. I talked about this with Dave Mohel, the President of BlueSkin Solutions, a comprehensive communications strategy firm and the company that runs radio row at the largest annual gathering of the political right, the Conservative Political Action Conference (CPAC). He was able to break down the market and the way that incentives and profit motive are a driver in this relationship as well as discuss the cautious attitude that I had run into when at CPAC visiting radio row.

> There are many reasons for radio shows to be cautious. Their business model relies heavily on people being in their cars or office who are captured audiences or people tuning in for local news and sports information. Technology has taken away their audiences faster than could have been predicted. Plus, the overall downturn in the economy has scared away advertisers. As a result, the profits in the radio industry are small and budgets are cut. What we provide is a way for those hosts and stations to get amazing content and increase their brand while keeping their spending down. The events' sponsors and guests have an opportunity to reach millions of people in earned (free) media in a short amount of time. So everyone wins. Shows get access to guests and content that may not have otherwise at no cost to them; the event sponsors get what amounts to hundreds of hours of free ads for their event.[23]

What Dave didn't mention was that he also operates as kind of an air traffic control while at CPAC. He helps get more people on the air, good people, which as he said is good for both the conference and the radio shows. The win-win has kept the radio row at CPAC growing for years and kept CPAC continuing to hire Dave and BlueSkin solutions.

All of these relationships are high stakes, and profit motives affect the way that information is presented. Talking heads aren't being paid to be neutral observers. They aren't paid by the show at all, but since they are getting something out of this, it's is important to pay attention to their profit motive. Figuring out the profit motive of talking heads is fun and interesting. (Unless they just wrote a book—then that's easy to figure out.) Being on TV or radio is not actually that easy—it costs a lot. Why would someone put up with working on someone else's time frame, answering their questions, showing up at their studio, paying for the transportation to their studio, wearing heavy make-up, possibly missing dinner with their family, putting their kids to sleep, or potentially embarrassing themselves forever in front of everyone if they screw up? However, those sacrifices are just scratching the surface on pointing to the fact that there is a profit motive in being on TV. In fact, some people will now even pay to be on shows.

Show Sponsorship

The big market for pay-for-play media is the radio. I personally worked for a group that sponsored a show during the ObamaCare debate. At the time I wasn't senior enough in the organization to be privy to all of the conversations, but I know it wasn't cheap.

What did we get for it? Our organization's research was used when appropriate, and our boss was on the air whenever they could fit him in as well as other guests that our organization had handpicked. I am sure that the radio show that we had "sponsored" had veto authority, but their motivation is to say "yes." After too many "no's" money tends to dry up as the value lessens.

I bring up the organization that I worked with to show that this is rampant in media, but we were just flirting with the market because we weren't one of the larger organizations where this type of market manipulation is standard practice. The larger groups are warring over the big players. Rush Limbaugh and Sean Hannity were receiving around $2 million and $1.3 million respectively back in 2011 from the Heritage Foundation, while their competitor Americans for Prosperity was paying Mark Levin, and FreedomWorks was paying Glenn Beck.

In a 2011 article from *Politico,* one of the people in charge of one of these programs gave an interview discussing the "sponsorships." Genevieve Wood, Heritage's vice president for operations and marketing, said:

We approach it the way anyone approaches advertising:
Where is our audience that wants to buy what you sell?
And their audiences obviously fit that model for us. They
promote conservative ideas and that's what we do.[26]

Should we all be scared that the media is going to brainwash us all into supporting a certain group just to make more money? No. Not at all. Profit Motive keeps them from this. If the Heritage Foundation all of the sudden decided to support something antithetical to where Rush Limbaugh is on an issue, Rush would likely refuse to talk about it and possibly even drop them as a sponsor.

In fact, Glenn Beck dropped one of his show's sponsors when that corporate sponsor took bailout money, largely because of Congressional pressure.[27] Since these shows have faithful listeners, they can't change their policy position just because of a sponsor's whim. So their profit motive is to only to take money from people that they agree with.

There is also another side to the profit seeking of a media business that has an effect that changes their programming, but is very hard to control. "Profit," in this situation, which we discuss in more detail at the end of the book, isn't all about money, and when it is, it isn't always about "money now." Faithful radio show listeners might not be alright with a show host changing their view on an issue. That means that a radio show's audience can act as an anchor for the show's direction. If Rush's audience is largely supporting a candidate like Ted Cruz, but Ted Cruz does something that Rush finds appalling, Rush is unlikely to suddenly oppose the Senator. This causes the masses to rule a bit more than they would because of the financial motivation to sell to the audience.

Again, for both sides of this equation, the radio show sponsors and the radio shows, an understanding of why Rush Limbaugh might discuss a Heritage Foundation report and Glenn Beck a FreedomWorks report can be helpful when attempting to distill the truth or some relative truth from a conversation. When you can figure out why Rush is quoting a certain report, or understand that he is unlikely to quote a Cato study, a libertarian competitor of the Heritage Foundation, unless it is the only report that he can use to make his point, the "news" on radio talk shows start becoming a lot easier to understand.

One show that I am a frequent guest on has an interesting profit motive to figure out. I am frequently asked to participate on the *Thom Hartmann Program*. His show appears on Russian Television America. It is a channel funded by Russia. I have been a follower of the channel for a long time because before Russia invaded Ukraine it had some excellent libertarian-ish financial shows, including a great show that spent a fair amount of time discussing Bitcoin. However, once they invaded Ukraine, Russia tacked the channel in a different direction. There the whole time was Thom Hartmann, so if you don't look too far into it you might assume that he was bending to the Russian viewpoint. However, after being on the show weekly for about a year, it was fairly obvious that Thom and his show weren't being edited. It turns out that as a part of his contract negotiations he only uses RT studios, and they don't have editorial control.

That said, he is on RT. So, it still warrants a deeper look. While it might make sense for Thom to pay attention and edit or fight any messages against Russia, his show is big enough and legitimizes RT in a way that they can't buy. Therefore, it is in RT's profit motive for Thom to continue his full independence. It is an interesting symbiotic existence and profit motive.

Thom is an entrepreneur who, in addition to his shows, has founded several successful businesses and has lived and worked with his wife, Louise, and their three children on several continents. His radio show is the #10-ranked radio show which is available in 500 million homes worldwide according to *Talkers Magazine*. He is a *New York Times* best-selling author and has written a total of twenty-four books. His TV show, *The Big Picture*, is also fully owned by Thom and produced at RT studios and is broadcast into more than 600 million homes.

Thom and I don't see eye-to-eye on public policy, economics, or the basic ways that the world works. What we have in common, though, is that we both care about these things, and we are willing to listen to others and continue to grow and learn.

Thom doesn't have the large sponsors that Rush, Sean, Glenn, or Mark have, which is also a normal characteristic of shows on the left, but Thom's listeners and followers are a devoted and large group. That means that RT is happy to have Thom on their program, and the Sirius XM is happy to carry Thom's daily radio show to provide valuable programming to their listeners.

Thom's TV show and his radio show are as different as night and day. I have learned a lot from being on both of Thom's shows. Thom's market is a devout group of progressive listeners, and he has people like me on almost as a curiosity.

I am routinely asked to be on Thom's political panel for his TV show. The Wednesday panel is the feisty one, and that is the one that he often asks me to be on. The first time was another valuable lesson about media, entertainment, and of course Profit Motive.

I got the list of issues at 3:00 p.m. the day of the show, I was told to show up at the studio at 6:30 and we were going live at 7:00 p.m. I was warned that they sometimes like starting people off on their Monday political panel which is softer, slower, and more friendly. I turned it down, and said that I was ready.

I wasn't. The list of issues that I received was ten bullet points long and ranged in issues from money in elections, to immigration, to unemployment, and more. I looked at the list wide-eyed. Before the first show I had given myself some time, so I was ready when I arrived at the studio. In the green room, the waiting room, I was again warned that this was going to be a fast-paced debate.

When we moved out of the green room there were two chairs. I had the first chair and another right-leaning talking head had the second chair. Thom started the introduction to the segment and the producer rolled our chairs into place while the camera was on Thom. As soon as Thom introduced us, the other talking head started yelling at Thom and Thom started yelling back—I almost laughed. This was going to be an intense thirty minutes. After a few minutes, I jumped in and Thom responded by quacking at me with money in his hand taunting me asking, "Is this free speech? Quack, quack, quack!"

The whole thing still makes me smile.

Before the end of the segment I was able to argue with both of them at full speed, but I definitely had not been ready at the beginning despite the several warnings I had received throughout the process. Thom was giving his viewers value by showing that he could handle the attacks from the right. Not only could he handle the attacks, but he could handle two of them at once. It was a little bit like a carnival strong man showing that he can out-lift anyone in the crowd. It was a spectacle, and because of that need to provide a spectacle the debate needed more over the top than a normal political.

The problem right now is the "Profit Motive." It used to be that prior to 1987 (from The Federal Communications Act of 1927 until 1987) the belief was that the airwaves were a natural monopoly. Therefore, they are owned by 'We The People,' and we were going to grant limited availability. Thus the monopoly.

So, we were going to grant those monopoly rights to certain organizations based on whatever criteria we come up with, which is mostly first-come - first-serve, and once they have those monopoly rights in order to maintain those monopoly rights: Okay like you are 1350 am and you've got that for Washington DC forever—and how you maintain that monopoly you program in the public interest and the definition—and that was put into law in the 1920s—and what was broadly understood to be programing in the public interest.

Most people misunderstood and thought it was things like public service announcements. You know, run an ad for mothers against drunk driving. That was thrown into the mix, but mostly those are just used when people cancel advertising, principally radio stations they got an extra spot they stick a PSA in there.

This was the principal way the program radio and television stations program. The public interest was with something called news, and so the news divisions of ABC, CBS, NBC, they all lost money. They had bureaus all over the world. They lost money in the abstract, they lost money as a standalone entity, but arguably they weren't actually losing money. What they were really doing was paying the cost of the monopoly—the access to the public airwaves.[28]

—Thom Hartman on Profit Motive and news
From an interview I held with him on October 13, 2016

Of course, Thom wins every debate—it's his show. He controls the topics, the questions, the framing, and of course the clips that he has ready, but what he gives his guests is the ability to appear in front of a very large audience. His audience is valuable enough that getting beaten up is worth it. I am now on the program almost every week, and it has helped me develop my career. Like One America News, Thom's guests are not paid to be on the show, but he is able to fill up his political panels whenever he wants because of the value that his audience provides guests.

Because of his influence in media and in part his opposition to my political leanings, I wanted to talk to Thom about "Profit Motive" and his thoughts on the idea. So, one day after I was on his show we talked, and he shared some thoughts with me. One question I asked him was to get an answer about something that actually started during a commercial break a few weeks earlier. During the commercial break we spoke about my ideas about profit motive, and he quipped, "I don't just care about money. I care about family, others, and the environment too." He then laughed because a producer spoke into his earpiece saying, "Okay, hippy, we are back in thirty seconds."

So, I started the conversation by fully explaining "Profit Motive" and focusing on the point that profit isn't just money, and then he responded to my question about his Profit Motive in business and for his shows:

> I know Louise and I, with every business that we started, everything we've done in our lives, we've always had three criteria: Number one. Can we have a lot of fun doing it? Number two. Can we make a living at it? And number three: Can we change the world, the process, for the better? And, so you know every venture that we have undertaken has been congruent with those life values.

I have spoken with a lot of different entrepreneurs from a lot professions, and while most can't articulate their thoughts as well as Thom, the successful entrepreneurs almost always think the same way he does. Some, maybe not as liberal as Thom, would put making money first on their list, but because of the long hours, stress, and effort that goes into building a company, if entrepreneurs didn't have profit motives outside of money they would fail at an even higher rate than they do already.

Thom is different from most, and that is probably what helps drive his success. With a radio show that is on five days a week and a TV show that is broadcast five days a week as well. Thom is in his own constant cycle of research-show-research-show that makes his days long and his nights short. The first time that I fully understood his schedule was the first time that I did both his radio show and his TV show. He starts his radio show at 12:00 noon and is on the air for a full three hours. He then grabs a quick lunch and starts preparing clips, research, and guests for his 7:00 p.m. TV show. He has a full team of people around him to help, but captaining that schedule and being ready to sit in front of a microphone and TV camera is a draining task.

It is obvious that Thom does put a lot of weight into the "hippy" profit centers that he had already identified with his wife Louise.

If Thom wanted to make more money he might be able to find a sponsor like his colleagues with shows on the political-right (if he was willing to shill for their message). If Thom wanted to make more money he could likely move his show to CNN instead of Russian Television, but then he would also give up the ability to have full editorial control. Thom lives up to the goals that he and Louise have set for themselves.

Because Thom puts weight on something besides money first, does that mean that he is more trustworthy, though? I don't think so, but that is because profit is profit. He is still getting something out of doing his shows and earning any type of profit that shapes what he is doing and how he acts. I happen to know Thom fairly well, and I couldn't have more respect for the man and his shows. I personally think that he is very trustworthy. However, because of his motivation to "change the world," he uses research that often comes from one specific worldview instead of attempting to show all sides of an issue.

This choice is completely his prerogative. He shouldn't have to show up on a show every day and present information that I feel will make the world a better place. He has built his brand and his platform to present his message. Thom is getting rich, although it might not be the same type of "rich" as Rush Limbaugh or Sean Hannity. But his incentives are the same as theirs.

Media Bias

It is a common theme on the political right that the media is heavily biased to the left. From the political left, there is almost a palpable hate that emanates from any of their conversations about Fox News because of the network's bias to the right. These beliefs and accusations are deeply felt on both sides, and are each correct in their own ways. However, if the bias is real why does the bias exist given the idea of Profit Motive? Or, are there other biases that are even more important?

Working with the political media machine for most of my career, writing for about a dozen publications, and appearing on at least four different television networks in that time, you start getting a sense for the pulse and tendencies of media. Most of my TV and writing experience has been for news organizations that have a center-right to far-right-leaning tendency. This view of media helps me appreciate the left-leaning media for the same reason that I like the right-leaning media. They each have a role, and all of the organizations I've written for are pretty straightforward about their worldview.

In fact, One America News, at least in the beginning, was explicit that their goal was to compete to the right of Fox News.

Given how Fox News is the dominant cable news channel and they tend to do more right-leaning programming and hire more right-leaning hosts than any other station, most of their previous competitors felt that the broadest market was to the left of Fox. This is the trap that people fall into if they if they don't ask what their clients want or attempt to understand what the people watching their channel get out of watching it.

One America News set out to compete with Fox News, and in just a few years they are reaching the levels of the Left-leaning media channels. They even almost received the privilege of hosting one of the debates during the presidential primary campaign even though they are only a few years old. One America's growth has been fast and substantial and helping to at least prove their business model. There is demand for media that doesn't lean left, and there might even be *more* demand for media that explicitly leans right. In fact, now that other organizations have seen the space that One America has quickly made for themselves, some of the other stations that had previously only focused on online programming and building their social media presence are now jumping into the conversation.

The popularity of Fox News, One America News, and their new competitors make it obvious that there is more going on than a so-called "Liberal Bias" of the media. It isn't just that Fox is an effective counterweight, or that Fox is actually centrist. The truth is that Fox is making more money, they are leading the market, and if stations wanted to make money, which is what should be assumed given the Profit Motive, then something else is causing their success.

There is unquestionably a left of center bias in the media. But it has less to do with media or a quest for profits. Reporters and producers for mainstream media are usually not given policy directives from media ownership. Where the real bias comes from is higher education. At most journalism schools, future newsroom staff is taught to look at the world through a liberal lens and are graded accordingly.

—Dave Mohel, BlueSkin Solutions
From an Interview I held with him on October 25, 2016

My personal hypothesis has always been that the types of people who are more likely to seek out jobs in the media are also most likely the people that like focusing and telling the stories of individuals. Dave Mohel builds on that hypothesis and points more toward the education that journalists usually go through. Dave is probably right. Teachers tend be more Left-leaning, and they also probably teach their student journalists to bring in a specific story about an individual to help tell the story. This forces a left lean into the programming.

This isn't just my thinking, though. One of the most complete looks into the bias of media agrees that there is a Left-leaning to most of the media. As Groseclose says:

> We measure media bias by estimating ideological scores for several major media outlets. To compute this, we count the times that a particular media outlet cites various think tanks and policy groups, and then compare this with the times that members of Congress cite the same groups. Our results show a strong liberal bias: all of the news outlets we examine, except Fox News' *Special Report* and the *Washington Times*, received scores to the left of the average member of Congress. Consistent with claims made by conservative critics, *CBS Evening News* and the *New York Times* received scores far to the left of center. The most centrist media outlets were *PBS NewsHour*, CNN's *NewsNight*, and ABC's *Good Morning America*; among print outlets, *USA Today* was closest to the center. All of our findings refer strictly to news content; that is, we exclude editorials, letters, and the like.[29]

Contrary to what Dave Mohel said is actually happening—or not happening—maybe there should be a verdict from the top to move to the right, or at least attempt to moderate. Given the success of Fox News it is obvious that viewers respond to this different approach and Profit Motive would suggest that the channels should change accordingly. (This is what MSNBC has explicitly done in recent years.) Maybe more important to understand is that if the current market incumbents don't make a change it is likely that they will be left behind as the market corrects back toward the middle—all in the name of seeking profit.

Of course there will always be a market for media that leans left, like Thom Hartmann's shows, but given the numbers of Fox News as compared to their cable competitors, it is obvious where the demand is.

So, there is a media bias, and the bias is Profit Motive. Is that okay? Is that what we are destined to live with? As a part of my conversation with Thom Hartmann he asserted that the answer is no, "Because of the Profit Motive there has been a loss of what I would say is an essential part of our commons, which is an informed and educated populace."

Thom isn't wrong, I have even seen some of the older news stories exposing businesses in ways that we just don't often see anymore. However, the timeline is a problem for Thom because it is very possible that his observation is merely correlation instead of causation. In the early '80s the television markets were changing, and they were changing rapidly because cable news was making its appearance. The 24-hour news cycle had begun. Now people who wanted news could have access anytime they wanted. The market wasn't flooded with options at first, and the first 24-hour news option, CNN, was not too much of a departure from its network news predecessors. And, that is largely the way it stayed until the early 90s.

There wasn't much competition, and Fox News didn't jump into the game until 1996. Competition meant that the war had begun. Fox immediately began fighting for their share of the market, and CNN reacted, and now we have seen this competition change the whole news landscape.

Like social media, the user/viewers are not the payers. The users and viewers are the product that the stations sell. So when the competition began between CNN and Fox the competition was playing out in two ways. First, news started becoming more entertaining. CNN had hosted a political debate show, *Crossfire*, since the early '80s, but the debates became even more entertaining. What that means in a "news" sense is that facts give way to talking points and one-liners. It also means that the personalities have less of a reason to agree. Both factors combine for a show that is more entertaining for viewers to watch, but it might not convey as much information as it did in the past.

The more important fight for shaping news was the battle over the money. The payers for news are the advertisers. Profit Motive is ever present, so it should be pretty obvious that businesses don't like paying for advertising on a channel that is going to reveal them through some sort of an exposé or use their advertising money to put time, money, and resources into stories that aren't entertaining and might lose viewers—like news. The end result is an industry that is unlikely to expose business corruption with any veracity, and if a station did such an exposé it might be valuable to check the station's own business interests for ruining the reputation of a potential client. Other countries have attempted to solve this issue by at least attempting to strip out the Profit Motive.

Thom Hartmann said:

> Now there is a way that countries deal with this if you look at Germany or France or England. There are dozens of other examples as well, but those are well known to Americans. The way that they dealt with that was that instead of saying to commercial broadcasters you must carry news, they said we will set up an entity that is funded by government, that operates within government, but operates independently of government.

In some ways I agree with Thom. I think that it is obvious to even casual observers that the news is less about news and more about entertainment than it was in the days of black-and-white cabinet televisions. However, the solution is not to ignore Profit Motive"; the solution is to embrace it. If news is too boring, not enough people will watch it—leading back to Thom's fear of an uneducated and ill-informed populace. We are seeing the other side now. There's too much entertainment, but information is power, and there is also demand for real news.

Profit Motive should also be seen as the correcting influence in this equation. Like a lot of markets, when something new is introduced the market, it usually goes too far and then corrects, over-corrects, and finally settles back into some new normal. The news market is just moving through these iterations slowly. They have gone too far, but we are starting to see the first signs of market correction, as well. One America News has several talk shows that are far- and very-far-right leaning. However, for the rest of the day they have news readers reading domestic news stories that seem to be coming directly from the Associated Press's news feed. Therefore, they are right down the middle and a great source of pure news for the majority of the day. The same can't be said about Fox, CNN, or MSNBC. OAN is still growing though; we will see whether they change when they reach the scale of the others, or continue to forge what appears to be a path closer to the news that Thom Hartmann and many others yearn for.

News Sites

In the last few years there has been a lot of experimentation in news rooms across the country, and these changes are most evident on news websites. This part of normal market growth is in the face of technological changes, but it has sometimes made it harder to figure out where exactly money is coming from.

If you are watching TV and they take a commercial break, it used to be obvious that the commercial is paid for and is helping to support the programming. However, now companies are increasingly paying for product placement in TV shows. I haven't personally noticed it infiltrate the news yet, but at some point there is likely to be a first time.

Websites are not much different. When we visit websites and see the ads on the sidebar of the webpage, we think that is what is funding the website. These ads are intriguing. Sometimes people pay just to have their banner seen, but that type of ad only pays pocket change in return for thousands and thousands of views. Others pay slightly more than pocket change, but users have to click on the ad for the site to collect money. For a site to make money from their ads they have to generate a lot of traffic. That is why we are often inundated with headlines like the "twelve best ways to recycle business plans" or the even more clickbait like "Women shares her dinner table—you won't believe what happens next."

In other words, the content begins to follow the search for money, and that often means more entertainment vs. news and information. And even then sites are currently finding it hard to make money. Sites like Gawker, Huffington Post, and Salon have all gone through fairly substantial and public downsizing recently and as fewer people click on ads. That trend is likely to continue.

There is another way that some sites have tried: paywalls. Sites like *The Wall Street Journal* are locking up many of their posts and only allowing paying subscribers access to the information, but this has proved tough as well. Many web users are accustomed to "free news," so when they run into a gated article they just search out a new source for similar information. It might not be at the same quality as *The Wall Street Journal*, but free is often much cheaper and more efficient than getting a subscription that you might only use infrequently. The paywall gives new sites a way to maintain their "news" and not bend as much to the will of advertisers that aren't needed in the same numbers since readers are paying.

However, the subscription part gets in the way since payers/readers/members have their own Profit Motive, and that means that they need the need to get an amount equal to the subscription cost that is above and beyond what they can get from "free" sites. It is a hard sell.

There is one last version of "news" sites trying to replace their incentive to make money from advertisers to one of making money from readers that might prove to be even more effective than a paywall: tipping. What if you could "tip" an author or site for a good article? A tipping system would avoid the use or at least the overuse of click bait titles, so that users aren't let down after reading the story. A tipping system would put the reader back in the driver seat. Readers wouldn't have to support every article that a news organization puts out in order to benefit from the few that they want to enjoy. They would merely reward a news source for the articles that they found helpful. This would work well for reporting on something like the safety of child products too. For instance, if a company that produces child goods is advertising on a website, that website is unlikely, or least less likely, to write a story that exposes safety concerns about their product. However, if it is parents paying for the content, then the incentive, the Profit Motive of the site, is to publish articles and information that parents will find most helpful—like exposing the safety concerns of a particular product.

In fact, this was already tested on at least one website, and while the technology still has some bugs that are being worked out I could picture this being the way that the incentives are fully corrected in the future of news delivery.

However, for now, the primary way to remove the incentive to bow to the interests of advertisers are donors. The closest news'ish organization that currently operates this way is PBS, but I know several prominent new organizations on the right that received startup capital that was intended as more of a donation than an investment. One other way that is currently gaining traction, and includes some good profit-based incentives, are the several crowd-funding platforms like Kickstarter and Patreon that allow people to advertise their ideas pre-production and allow the users of the platforms to pre-pay for the product. By doing this the websites are letting their users build a their own dreams rather than making money from advertisers that might not want certain products or documentaries produced. These websites have shifted their profit motive.

So, Is There Any News in Here?

The point of this chapter is that you always have to keep your eyes and ears open. Identifying the profit motive of your news sources can be very beneficial to the outcome of how you feel about a certain news event.

You shouldn't trust the talking heads, you shouldn't trust the headlines, you shouldn't trust that the absence of news means that everything is fine, you shouldn't trust that "news" is delivered without bias, and you shouldn't trust that all news is biased in one direction.

It is also obvious that profit motive manipulates the news; it is one of the most important effects of profit seeking that we can recognize as individuals and as a society.

Thom Hartmann is right when he talks about the idea that a move from informational news to entertaining and bought-and-paid for news is a shift toward a less educated and informed public. But the solution isn't as easy as bringing back the Fairness Doctrine or even creating our own BBC. As Thom knows well, we kind of have that in America. We have PBS and NPR. When they were started they were funded by the government, but because their programing was popular, Sesame Street for example, the motivation of politicians was to spend money on other things—like bridges to nowhere and $500 hammers. Now NPR only receives less than 10 percent of its budget from the federal government. The rest is funded by the private sector, and now the public/private organization is competing with Thom and his radio show.

That isn't good for Thom because NPR has the aura of impartiality because of its roots as a fully government-funded organization. Now that they operate with so little funding from the government, they are on the prowl for more advertisers and supporters, which means that they have moderated their exposés and are now competing for Thom's audience, which is looking for entertainment.

The best way is to get advertisers out of the way and just have the consumers pay directly for the news. That might look like the beta project that I have referred to as tipping. Or, it might look like something that we haven't yet seen. Maybe Netflix starts by hosting a weekly news show. Their subscribers would benefit and profit from additional content, and they would benefit by providing yet another feature to their subscribers—the unbiased, by advertisers, news programming.

There is also more than just advertising that biases news, and that is fame and messaging. In professions like politics if you appear on TV, you are more respected. I discussed earlier the reasons that talking heads might want to appear, but we only started scratching the surface because television and radio appearances helps people raise money by lending credibility to their message. It also provides a campaign surrogate, or similar position, which is the ability to drive home a planned message. So even more than just helping to brand themselves, a TV spot isn't necessarily about sharing information: it is about the appearance, the message delivered in that appearance, and how well it was delivered. All of this influences the Profit Motives to make the appearance less about sharing information with the viewers and more about the guest themselves.

Once you start seeing the profit motive bias in media, it is hard to un-see. For instance, I can no longer watch CNN for more than just a few minutes without wanting to throw something at the screen. As a part of my early career I watched CNN everyday all day, and they definitely have a bias. The part of the bias that frustrates me the most is that they attempt to deny that they have a bias. The other channels have their biases as well, but handle this differently. Most on Fox are explicit, and other channels don't try to hide their bias as much as CNN. CNN is still a good channel in many ways, but I can't un-see their bias, which dramatically effects the way that they portray every story.

But seeing Profit Motive is more important than attempting to stay blinded. Pay attention to who is getting paid, who is paying them, and what that means to the information that is in the news. It's pretty easy to figure out: they run ads for them in between news segments.

PROFIT MAN

The people that are on TV are making a profit, but Profit Man is the guy that is usually sitting in the penthouse suite that owns the channel. Profit Man is deciding who people see, what the programs are like, and is selling the ads that are run in between the shows.

Profit Man understands that people are watching his shows 24 hours a day and 365 days a year which means that he has a lot of time to profit. If Profit Man is too greedy, he might lose a viewer, which means that he loses 365 days of opportunities to sell and he loses a recruit that might bring in another viewer. Profit Man is the puppeteer of media, but he needs viewers to sell to. So, Profit Man is continually walking a thin line, but because of the high cost of losing a viewer, Profit Man is likely to err on the side of the viewer.

Profit Man also doesn't necessarily care about the news, or what it is in the news. What Profit Man cares about is that the news is interesting and entertaining. That has an effect on the way that stories are told, and it has an effect on the order and weighting of stories, but Profit Man doesn't care about stories or politics as much as he does about how viewers or listeners will think about the stories.

5

Profit-Driven Health Care for All

SITTING IN AN EXAM ROOM WITH MY WIFE who was eight months pregnant and experiencing Braxton Hicks contractions, the doctor suggested another test. My wife looked at me, I looked at my wife, and then I looked at the doctor and asked, "What will your recommendation be if the test results are positive?"

Her answer was, "Take it easy."

So, I then asked, "Given her current contractions, what would be your suggestion without a positive test result?" She, without any sense of irony, said, "Taking it easy."

I looked back at my wife, and we talked about the options right in front of that doctor. Option "A" was to leave the exam room, go home, and rest. Option "B" was to spend a few hundred additional dollars, take another stressful test, and be told to do the same thing that the free option had already suggested.

The system is broken. Education, logic, and common sense are no longer in control inside of the exam room. The profit motive in health care has largely been about getting patients better and keeping them healthy. However, as the system has lost cohesion the profit in the system has morphed, and it now can come from things like spending less time with clients, prescribing drugs that the doctor might not agree with prescribing, and even not seeing some patients because they might cost the doctor more than they are paid.

The primary problem for the average person is that we are no longer the clients. We aren't paying the bills, and most of the time the group that we are paying isn't even the one paying the doctor. That means that the profit motive isn't necessarily to treat the patient well; the profit motive is more about treating the payer well, and in this case "profit" usually means avoiding being fired, ostracized, fined, or sued. Therefore, doctors are often working in a way that makes the most sense for the hospital that is their employer, the insurance company that they are billing, or to defend themselves against a legal system that seems to consider doctors guilty from the start.

This is not the doctors' fault. Doctors become medical doctors to treat people and make them healthy. Even given the high salaries of some of the specialties, after figuring in the many years of education, the long hours, and the liability issues, being a doctor isn't as lucrative as it appears. And sometimes when a doctor looks like they are siding with a hospital over the patient, it's only because they are attempting to navigate the convoluted economic relationships to save the patient money. As one of my physician friends, Dr. Keith Smith, routinely says, "We need to advocate for our patients. I didn't go into health care to fix people, make them healthy, and then bankrupt them."

Dr. Smith decided that he couldn't do enough as an advocate within the system, so he innovated and started his own surgery center, which I'll discuss later in the chapter. Many other doctors see what is wrong with the system and are just trying to do their best, but the incentives in the system are against them at every stage of the game.

I have worked on health-care policy for a little more than a decade, and the most frustrating part of the public policy fight is that the people that I largely fight against all propose legislation that they sell by villainizing doctors, but their solutions almost always break down the patient-physician relationship even more than it already is, which eventually makes the problem even worse. The end result is that it is often a twenty-eight-year-old government bureaucrat is practicing medicine at the safety of their desk with no medical training. The more and more that doctors have been villainized, the more the government has taken away their decision-making privileges. This is sad.

The answer isn't just to give the doctor autonomy, though. The right solution is to empower the patient. We should let them participate in making decisions about their health, and let the patient control the money. When the patient controls the money they make different decisions.

When my wife and I were in that exam room, we were getting ready to welcome our first kid into the world. We were scared. We would have done anything for our soon-to-be-born infant. However, we were also broke, and we had a health-care plan that, until we reached the deductible, would charge us for any tests. Because of the decision we made, we saved money, we saved the system money, and there was no increased risk to our baby because the solution to the reason we were there was the same with or without another medical test. The problem for the doctor is that they needed to check off a liability box and a profit box. The doctor didn't hide the results from us, but it was also obvious that we were one of the few families asking questions instead of writing checks to someone with an overwhelming information advantage over us.

Like the other areas that we have looked at, profit motive is everywhere in health care. When done right, profit motive can create an efficient system that can provide quality health care at affordable prices. Done wrong, and with reckless government intervention, health-care plans can leave patients without care despite overpaying for an insurance policy that does more to protect the hospital than the patient.

Making Hospitals Rich and Patients Poor

Hospitals are companies, hospitals are companies, hospitals are companies! That means that they are in business to make a profit. If they aren't functioning in a way that will make a profit, their board is not fulfilling their fiduciary duty. Even nonprofit hospitals are in business to make a profit, and their profit is tax-free, which gives them a competitive advantage over their rivals. And, since the main cost variable in a hospital are the patients, the incentive structure such as raises/promotions/time-off are usually set up to give the individual employees at the hospital even more of a reason to save money on the backs of the patients. There are lots of pieces that go into making a profit, but spending extra money on patients is not one of them. Figuring out ways to spend less money is the goal.

Profit isn't bad, but because many in public policy view hospitals more as charities than as profit centers they often fail to understand the effects of their laws on the market. The results on the market have been that hospitals are taking over. They are becoming government-funded monopolies that are running up prices without regard for the laws of supply or demand. But the failure of hospital business practices to be regulated by market forces is merely a symptom. The disease that needs to be cured are the government laws that allow this perverse market to continue malfunctioning.

In Virginia, for instance, we have a law that limits the amount of operating tables that a surgical facility can have. The law is called Certificate of Need (CON), and hospitals love the law. First, hospitals have the majority of existing beds. Second, hospitals often have their own lobbyists to make sure that nobody else can compete with them. Third, hospitals have enough capital and control of the surgeons to pressure competitors to sell. Fourth, because of lobbying at the federal level, hospitals are often paid more for the same surgery as an outpatient surgery center would receive.

One outpatient surgery center that I know well in Virginia had to fight hard for their right to treat patients less expensively than the local hospital that they had recently separated from. The fight wasn't about quality; most of the same surgeons were operating at both places. The fight was about the hospital guaranteeing their profit center, seeking their profit motive, because the cost of surgery at the surgery center was about 20 percent of what the hospital was charging.

Laws like CON help line the pockets of hospitals, for-profit and nonprofit alike, with money, but they also distort the system and force patients to pay more than a healthy market would allow. It makes sense that as a business hospitals would fight with government to maintain their competitive advantage. And, since the hospitals control most of the beds and employ many of the physicians, and that number is consistently increasing, it also makes sense that many doctors fail to stand against the laws. Politicians are in this same category, given the fact that hospitals can afford lobbyists and can line political pockets with donations. Moreover, dissenting voices are often sparse and unorganized, and no politician wants to be labeled "bad for hospitals."

Given that all of the incentives in the current seem to align in a way that moves away from the patient, it's easy to be depressed about the system. So the next step for many public policy people is to conclude that the government should control the hospitals. But installing government control doesn't remove the profit motive of any of the individuals in the system or restore the patient-physician relationship in a way that would correct that profit motive; it's merely burying their head in the sand and wishing the problem away. If government control were the answer, the VA health system would be flawless. The solution is already out there and is starting to transform the market, and it is profit motive based. The solution is entrepreneurship and because of the high margins that hospitals are making over and above the market, they have a created a huge target for entrepreneurs to come in and provide better care at lower, sometimes a lot lower, prices.

Paycheck Policy

Our current health-care system is an employer-based model. Because of a quirk in public policy, bad war-time economic policy, employer-sponsored health care became a part of our economy. Fast forward a few decades and employer-sponsored health care now gets a tax break that would make other industry lobbyists blush and gives the employer-based market an almost unbeatable competitive advantage over private plans. The tax break is called the employer exemption, which means that employers can write off everything they pay toward an employee's health care. So, if an employee pays 15 percent in taxes this means for every dollar that the employer spends on health care, the employee gets approximately $0.15 free in insurance. And, conversely, the employer gets to provide a full dollar in benefits instead of the $0.85 cents that they would provide without the exclusion. Therefore, because of this large tax break, which is even larger for the highest-paid employees, the incentive is to forego pay increases in favor of more health care.

This is one of the reasons many unions have such good health care. When they are negotiating with the company an increase in health-care spending looks like a bigger win than it actually is to both sides.

It isn't just the company and the employee that think that this is good idea. Insurance companies understand tax policy too. They understand that the majority of their clients are getting a 10 to 15 percent discount on their product. Therefore, if the insurance company provides even 90 percent of what they should, the employees will think they are getting a good deal.

From there the problem gets worse. Since the employees aren't paying for the insurance directly, they aren't really the customer: the employer is. And as more and more doctors are hired by hospitals, the insurance company isn't paying the doctor, either; they are paying the hospital. That means that standing between the patient and the physician are at least four intermediaries, and in most cases it's even more once you include billing companies, lawyers, and other third parties that have added other layers to the health-care bureaucracy.

The problem that enables all of these layers is the original profit motive-driven decision that was made because of the exemption. First, if the exemption wasn't there, many employees might opt for an individual plan that would stay with them for years, giving the insurance company a larger profit motive to keep them healthy. Second, if the exemption wasn't there, employees would more likely push for insurance that offered them at least $1 dollar of value for a $1 dollar of cost. Third, to help maintain their value, the employees and employer would likely push for more accountability, as well as more service, but because they are only seeking a partial payback for their investment, it helps instead to drive up the cost because of less accountability. Fourth, and lastly, employees could be taking more money home and not sacrificing health care. They could also be making an even decision, without government intervention, between an extra dollar of health care vs. an extra dollar of take-home pay.

So removing the exemption is common sense. But it's also politically very hard.

> **A quick thought experiment:** If an individual has a total compensation package of $50,000 under an exclusion system and they are receiving $15,000 of that in health care, if and when the exclusion is lifted—assuming the employer doesn't change the compensation—the employee is likely to make the same amount of money, but it will feel like at least $1,500 less to them. What is the effect?

In the short run this isn't a situation that either the employee wants or the employer wants. It makes it hard to repeal. In fact, when Sen. John McCain was running against Sen. Barack Obama in 2008, McCain included the removal of the exemption as part of his health-care plan. Sen. Obama ran a campaign ad against the proposal (with around $100 million behind it) accusing John McCain of taxing health care and raising the taxes of employees.

It was a genius ad, but just because Sen. McCain's plan was a victim of a good political ad doesn't mean that it wasn't good public policy. Sen. McCain was trying to change the incentives in the system. It was good economics, but Sen. Obama and his team saw the weakness and understood that they could leverage the short-run profit motives of individuals while ignoring the benefits of the long-run changes that Sen. McCain had proposed. In fact, once he was elected the health-care bill that President Obama signed into law contained a variance on the removal of the exclusion: the Cadillac Tax.

This policy quibble/debate/attack provided me one of the more interesting things that I have learned in DC: academics from both side of the aisle aren't actually far away on the policies that they think are the right solutions. It is the political campaign that often gets in the way of the good public policy. But in the middle of a campaign the "Profit" to be gained is not in quibbling over policy. The "Profit" is attacking your opponent, and catching a Republican taxing people (despite the fact that his plan wasn't a net tax-raiser) was a political win.

While the ObamaCare Cadillac Tax is a sloppy way of accomplishing what economists in both parties identified as a need to accomplish, the tax helped restore an even playing field between bringing home an extra dollar in pay vs. adding an extra dollar in insurance.

The Right Way

There are doctors who are opting out. They are opting out of the broken system, and their numbers are growing. But doctors opting out one at a time hasn't created a large enough mass to shift the market substantially to beat the lobbyists and cronies.

The interesting thing to watch economically is a movement that started in Oklahoma about seven years ago, and, because of their successes, is now starting to move across the country and accelerate. The progress of the movement in changing the broken health-care system isn't fully understood, but given their pace of growth and the impact they have already made, saving patients and employers millions of dollars, a full understanding of their impact is only a few years away.

I know the first players in the movement well because together we formed a group to help increase the speed of the market's growth: The Free Market Medical Association. I don't work with the Association anymore since the group was growing faster than what I had time for, but because of their success the group is better and has continued to grow and accelerate in membership and its reach in educating those interested in the free market health-care movement.

The two other founders were Dr. Keith Smith, a cofounder of the Surgery Center of Oklahoma, and Jay Kempton, President of the Kempton Group Administrators, the founders of the modern free market health-care movement. Without these two individuals, it is likely that someone else would have identified the market that Dr. Smith and Jay Kempton identified, but it is unlikely that they would have solved the problem in a way as scalable or clean as they did.

Dr. Smith is an anesthesiologist who was fed up with the system. He wanted to do things differently. He wanted to restore the patient-physician relationship, and he wanted to be paid what he thought he was worth, not what the government thought he was worth. So, along with a Medical School buddy, Dr. Steve Lantier, they bought an old surgery center. Their first center was theirs; it was a blank slate and was theirs to run in the way they saw fit.

Almost immediately, salesmen started coming in to sell the two doctors, and new owners of a surgery center, on using their supplies, drugs, and prosthetics. A lot of money comes through a surgery center, and everyone wanted a cut. The salesmen know how to get into the front of the line—they offer the doctors money to use the supplies. The money is offered in different forms to avoid complication with the laws at any given time, but the money is there. But for Dr. Smith and Dr. Lantier, this type of transaction was not the way they wanted to practice medicine. If the transaction didn't benefit the patient (in this case kickbacks), their rule was to turn it down. That changed the negotiations. Now, they were talking about discounts instead of kickbacks—or just looking at the puzzled faces of salesmen who didn't understand why someone was turning down a bribe.

It didn't stop there. While they were building their surgery center's business, people called and ask about the cash price for services. Keith would call the people involved and ask what they wanted for a certain procedure, add in the supplies, and put together a price. Eventually, he put together a full list of prices. In fact, he is still building his list and his network of free-market doctors. The last time I had dinner with Keith I asked him about a procedure, and he brought out a book full of sticky notes to thumb through: it was his personal list, or what may be thought of as the guide book for the free-market medical movement.

So Dr. Smith had his list of prices, but he still wasn't really doing anything with the prices unless people asked. However, he was also frustrated that their surgery center's business wasn't growing as fast as he thought it would. He knew that his prices beat the hospitals since he was charging only a small percentage of their price. And, because of the smooth way that Dr. Lantier and Smith were running the surgery center, they had attracted the best doctors in the area, so they knew it wasn't their quality of professionalism that was a problem. Ruminating about his list of prices and his frustration, Dr. Smith decided to post the prices on the internet.

I have never spoken to Dr. Smith about his exact moment of doing this, but like most self-confident entrepreneurs and rabble rousers, I thought he'd probably kicked back in his chair and celebrated the silence before his phone started ringing off the hook. After all, he had just posted prices that were about 80 percent less than what the hospital down the street was charging.

But the phone didn't start ringing.

Actually, his business didn't really pick up that much. A few Canadians stumbled on the site, a few medical tourism travel agents found the site, and some uninsured people from other parts of the country found the site, but that was about it. Until Jay Kempton saw the prices.

Many Third Party Administrators (TPAs) have moved beyond being service driven to being product driven. No longer do they care about what is actually best for their client, but instead focus on how much revenue they can attract and retain through commissions, deals with networks and Pharmacy Benefits Manager (PBMs) pricing gymnastics. A significant chunk of their revenue is from charging a percentage of savings, a percentage of claims, or a percentage of subrogation recovery; all standard TPA functions. With this type of compensation structure, they are rewarded when claims are high and the Plan is performing poorly. Insurance carriers masquerading as TPA's are able to find even more ways of hiding their compensation (especially if they also own the network, the stop loss carrier, PBM. etc.)

Even though many of these revenue streams are considered standard industry practice, they are not transparent, nor are they in the best interest of the self-funded employer. The Employee Retirement Income Security Act of 1974 (ERISA) requires that self-funded employers use Plan assets only for reasonable expenses. The inability to quantify the exact compensation paid to their TPA puts employers in a non-compliant position with ERISA and may violate the employer's fiduciary responsibility to the

Plan. The Department of Labor, and the beneficiaries of these Plans, are starting to take notice.

My company charges a flat, per employee per month fee for all of our services because my loyalty lies only with my client, and I only get paid by my client. Kempton also works directly with free market providers to help our clients save money, while providing enhanced benefits to their employees. This work with free market providers has saved our clients more than $32 million in claims costs in just a few years, while being entirely up front and transparent in our own business. So why isn't Kempton the most famous TPA in America? To be honest, because change is hard and most people think there must be a 'catch.'

Buyers of healthcare (employers and patients) need to stand up to the third parties and demand transparency. The system will only change when the black hat hospital systems, TPAs, insurance companies, brokers, networks, and all of the other players, are forced to change their ways, and the buyers know what they are buying, at what cost, and can determine what the value is. Employers are starting to learn, but the public at large still hasn't gotten the joke that the American system is not free market, and that they are being lied to about why costs are so high.

—Jay Kempton, Kempton Group Administrators
From an interview I held with him on December 20, 2016

Jay's Kempton Group Administrators is a third-party administrator: they do the administrative work for companies that "self-insure." They help create plans, they negotiate with hospitals, they do just about everything except take the risk—or the profit—from insurance. The self-insured companies pay them to manage the paperwork and the specifics because Jay's group are experts.

Jay, like Keith, was getting frustrated with the health care business. He was seeing prices increase, but the increases weren't tied to anything. They weren't tied to GDP, inflation, quality, supply, demand, or competition. But, nonetheless, the prices that his customers were being billed from the hospitals/providers kept rising. One of the worst aspects of this to Jay was the idea of the "discount" that the hospitals and other providers were providing. Hospitals would send Jay a bill for something like a hernia repair, one charge that he sent me as data was for $19,384. Then the hospital, supposedly recognizing the value of Jay's business and tough negotiation history, discounts the procedure for Jay's client to $14,974. That is a difference of over $4,000 dollars and total discount of 30 percent. From one magical number to another didn't seem like a discount to Jay, and he was fed up.

Then he stumbled on Keith's prices. The prices that Keith listed were way below the "discounted" rate that the hospital was charging. Jay was curious, although he was also suspicious. Jay was so suspicious that the prices weren't real that he asked for access to Keith's books!

After some vetting, Jay and Keith met. Jay was amazed that Keith's prices were the real deal, and they struck a deal that if an employee of one of Jays clients went to the surgery center, they could get the prices that Keith listed on the website. There was no discount, but the money had to be in Keith's bank almost like it was cash from the employee/patient.

Jay then went to his clients and showed them the numbers, and they set up a new plan. If any one of the employees in the new plan that Jay oversaw went to Keith's surgery center they wouldn't pay anything. The reason for this is simple. The highest price on Keith's price list today for a hernia repair is $7,450, and that is for the most minimally invasive and complicated procedure. That is more than 50 percent off the cost of the hernia repair in Jay's example data (and in the example data the patient would have paid less than half of that).

Jay had created a plan that was giving away health care for free, and the employers, his clients, loved him for it. His clients were now able to save thousands of dollars, save their employees money, and they were still getting good care—even better care. This was the birth of the modern free market in health care, and everyone involved in doing it was doing so for their own interests.

This was the birth of the modern free market At the beginning it was only really effecting a few thousand employees in the Texas-Oklahoma area.

Today, Jay has data and history on his side. He also has access to more surgery centers than just Keith's. Actually, he has put together his own list the Kempton Premier Providers. Together, they give Jay a full team of free-market specialists that can provide transparent, market-based prices to their clients. The potential savings is millions of dollars per client.

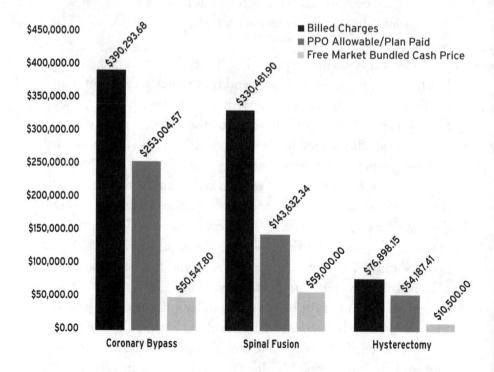

Jay's team showed me data from just one of their clients. The client had 2,800 employees, and in 6 months those employees had 472 procedures ranging from mammograms to a coronary bypass. They had the cost that they were billed by the hospitals, what the PPO allowable price was (the negotiated rate), and what the client could have paid if the employee had used one of the Kempton Premier Providers. The grand total that the client would have saved in just six months was slightly more than $1.5 million dollars, and their total payments would have added up to just shy of $900,000. That means that by avoiding the crony-driven hospitals, the client would have saved more than 50 percent and received the same quality or better care.

Talking about it now with Jay Kempton, when the market is now quickly expanding, but not yet the market norm, you might guess that he would be beating clients away. His company is growing, but it is still growing slowly. He told me:

> By working with surgery centers that embrace price transparency, post prices, and eschew the status-quo for free market principles, I have saved my clients millions of dollars. With a sales pitch like that you might think that it would bring the clients running, and I would say that business has picked up in recent years, but not as fast as the money we can save clients might warrant.
>
> There are of course many reasons for that, but part of it is just that people get comfortable. They don't like to make changes. We have developed ways—clients can just bolt on our product to theirs—to make a transition easier, but it is still a battle that we fight daily.

Profit Motive, sales, and economic trends are not things that can change a market overnight. However, what Jay and Keith are doing is catching on and, while the movement is still just starting to pick up speed, it has followers or practitioners across the country. There is a surgery center in California that lists its prices, there is one in Virginia, there one in Florida, one in Ohio, and now many others. Most of these surgery centers all have prices that are competitive with each other. And, when the prices do vary they often vary by less than a plane ticket, because many of the patients are willing to fly if the prices are much different.

Now that there are more surgery centers posting their prices, more and more people, business owners, and even government bureaucrats (who are a large part of the problem) are starting to see the light. For instance, the State of Oklahoma passed a bill in 2016 that allowed state employees to visit Dr. Smith's surgery center and benefit from the pricing, but the industry hasn't given in without a fight. Dr. Smith calls the industry a cartel, and I think that he's right. They have attempted to put him out of business several times, threatened him several times, and lobbied for bills to force the state to pay the hospitals' higher costs.

That hasn't stopped the growth and many government groups seem to be moving faster than private groups at this point of the movement, as Dr. Smith explains:

> Interestingly, self-funded public entities (municipalities, county, and state governments) are more drawn to the true savings that comes from dealing with non-price goug-ers than privately-held, self-funded health plans. While the local cartel of broker-carrier-hospitals has been very suc-cessful in maintaining their grip over private, self-funded health plans, the health plan of the State of Oklahoma came on board after only one year of dirty lobbying and Oklahoma County was one of the first to contract with us. I have come to believe that the relative lack of influence of brokers and consultants (whose income is largely driven by commissions derived from the carriers they represent) in the public sector explains this paradox.[30]

Dr. Smith further explained:

> There are now almost thirty facilities that have put these ideas into practice, customizing their models to fit their local market and introducing fresh new ideas from which our facility has benefited. Even more importantly, perhaps, are the innumerable times patients have printed prices from free market facilities and leveraged a matching deal from their local, otherwise price-gouging, hospital. While we are seeing this movement grow in numbers, the true effect the introduction of these market principles into this industry has had is much larger than anyone realizes.

These competitors didn't just pop up overnight though. Many of them were surgery center owners that were losing money to Keith. Others were losing money to the hospitals that control the health-care markets, and they were trying to figure out how to compete. Any way that you look at it, any of the new surgery centers are competition to Keith. Yet, Keith spends hours and hours talking with people who want to mimic what he and Steve Lantier have done at the Surgery Center of Oklahoma, and he does it for free. Keith has given these people access to his web designer, consulted—for free—with them through some of the bigger hurdles, and given them an ear when they just need to talk through personal issues while they make the transition.

This has actually been one of the things that Keith has been doing that I didn't understand. We touched on the fact earlier on in this book that capitalists aren't pro-competition, but Keith's action were almost the opposite. In fact, although I have known Keith and his story for about six years it wasn't until recently that I understood.

In Keith's way of thinking, he isn't helping his competitors; he is training his fellow soldiers. He is building an economic army to take down and reform the current health-care market with its artificially inflated prices that benefit everyone except the patient. Keith views these market incumbents as cartels that are going to attempt to take him out.

It took me awhile to understand, but Keith has a Profit Motive in teaching his competitors. As discussed, Jay's job would be easier because more people would understand that Keith isn't the odd one —he is just normal, and the rest of the market is so corrupt that Keith's prices looks out of place. And, as Keith talks about the increased number of people he sees, the bigger a target he is. For instance, the new law in Oklahoma is forecast to save the state $200 million. That is a lot of money, but let's assume that the measure only saves half that amount of money: it's still a lot money. This is money that would have gone to hospitals and money they won't have to pay their administrators bonuses, build on new wings, or buy out more physician practices to further corner the market. Keith is building his own army of Free Market Health-care data. It is hard to argue against the data. He explained his values and viewpoint about the competition to me in my interview with him:

> While many are drawn to applying the free-market principles to medical care delivery that I promote, many of the same individuals are initially confused about my willingness to share our strategies and even promote newcomers entering this marketplace, all of whom could be accurately characterized as my competitors.
>
> We are careful to distinguish our enemies from our competitors. We all know, after all, that the true enemies and bad guys in this cartelized industry are the crony, price-gouging institutional players who have purchased the right to bankrupt us individually and nationally, and the goons in DC who have auctioned off our liberties. While there are physicians who are part of the feeding frenzy at the taxpayer trough, the giant hospital systems

and those in corporate healthcare are the primary drivers of the cartel.

The guide for our business model is simply "The Golden Rule." By refusing to consider any agreement or proposal not consistent with exchange that is mutually benefi-cial, Dr. Lantier and I have steered clear of the traps and lures in which many physicians find themselves today. We remain committed to the concept of "maximum delivery of value," rather than "the maximizing revenue" approach that characterizes most of the industry. As there are more who are seeking value, there is plenty of work for those who choose to embrace this approach and therefore, why we are happy to promote our competitors in this new and vibrant marketplace.

Every time someone spends $3,000 instead of $30,000 for a life-changing surgical procedure at our facility or any number of others who have followed our lead, there arises the same shocking revelation of "What am I going to do with the $27,000 I didn't unnecessarily spend?" The power of this movement to shine the light on and eventually crush the US health cartels depends on this shocking revelation occurring hundreds or thousands of times a day. Another explanation for our championing new competitors: there is also safety in numbers![28]

Dr. Keith Smith on Teaching His Competitors
From an interview I held with him on January 2, 2017

It is almost like Keith is preparing himself for his own real world, "I am Spartacus!" moment.

This method doesn't stop with Dr. Smith, though. Josh Umber of Atlas, MD, teaches his competitors with the same zeal and energy that Keith does. Josh started a Direct Primary Practice in Kansas where patients pay a flat monthly fee to see Josh, or their doctor in the practice, whenever they want. It doesn't stop there either. His patients can text him, use Facetime, call, or even tweet him. Heck, Josh's prices are so cheap that I have thought about joining up my whole family, and I live in Virginia. (I don't want to if there would be any legal implications . . . but that's how good his prices are!)

Josh's practice, now more a robust business, is growing. He takes every opportunity he can to talk about it and how they built it with medical students, recent grads, frustrated family docs, and anyone else that will listen. And, just to make things easier for people, he has even created resources that aspiring free market doctors can use to start up their own practices.

The market is growing, and this time it has a chance because the people the movement are focused on building an even bigger army of supporters. They understand the profit motives of the incumbents are to maintain their markets. They don't want to give up power, and the money involved is too big for them to just walk away. The hospitals are going to fight.

The fight is worth it, though. Everyone talks about health care being too expensive. People refer to high prices of operations and the unbelievable cost of a hospital stay. Some say that "free" health care from the government is the solution, but that's just transferring who pays for it. The market is currently broken.

Once the incentives are corrected, the profit motives are addressed and taken into account, health care can be affordable. One of the most expensive procedures that Jay's data from the six month view of one company's health-care spending on 2,800 employees was for a cervical fusion. The original bill from the hospital was more than $330,000. I would agree that a bill that high is probably out of touch for the majority of people—including probably the doctors performing the operation. The discounted PPO rate that the client paid was still almost $150,000, and I would concede that for a health-care bill that is also likely too high a bill to consider it affordable. However, the Kempton Premier Provider price is $59,000. That is very expensive, but insuring against $59,000 instead of $150,000 is a lot more affordable, and most of the other procedures on the list are what many people would consider affordable if they weren't lining the pockets of insurance companies who were lining the pockets of hospitals.

Health care isn't going to be free-market based and affordable tomorrow, but tomorrow we will be closer to that goal because the profit motives are now aligning thanks to Keith, Jay, and everyone else who has joined their movement.

The Fight

As mentioned earlier, the cronies have not been receptive to the idea of reforming the cozy cartelized economy that they built around health care. But they currently don't have much choice, and that means that they are going to fight. Lobbyists are usually subtle, in large part because the politicians they're working with don't want to be seen as a part of the problem. So the profit motive for both is subtlety. Unfortunately, that wasn't working for the lobbyists in Oklahoma. So the lobbyists tried to outright stop the state from benefiting from Keith's low prices. Since they showed their hand, it was obvious that it was important. The lobbyists were forgoing anonymity to fight.

I might have expected a member on the Left not to support free market ideas, but in fact several on the left have been supportive in Oklahoma. The Left, at least some of the Left, in Oklahoma realize that since they have advocated for cheap, accessible, and high-quality care that they should probably support the guy providing that solution. The opposition ended up being a bought-and-paid-for Republican. By stopping the legislation that would have given Oklahoma State employees access to Keith's center, the politician showed he was working with the cronies. He was working to save his friends from losing what is forecast to be considerably more than $100 million. But the savings were too good, the pressure built up, and—although the cronies understood the importance of the bill—it is now obvious that they didn't understand the full ramifications, because the bill has passed. Now that the politicians have a taste of the savings, and the employees have it is well in the form of low or no copays and high quality care, they are going to have a hard time going back.

The hospital and insurance industries lost, and they know what they lost. But that doesn't mean they will go away quietly. The movement is rapidly growing, but it is still in its nascent stage and the time that the cronies have left to protect themselves is quickly going away, so their motivation, their profit motive, is to crush the movement now.

Attempting to think about the motives of everyone involved, what will the fight to save the crony profits look like?

I think that the answer is pretty simple: The lobbyists will fight to raise the amount of re-insurance that the self-insured must carry. Let's look at why. While Keith's posted prices work great for the uninsured, the growth in his business has come from self-insured businesses, and, even more specifically, some of the smaller Third Party Administrators. So cutting off a profit center would slow down the growth and give the large hospital systems even more of an opportunity to put the centers out of business. Additionally, raising the re-insurance rates could be done under the guise of making sure that the employees of the self-insured were protected.

The reason that this solution is a prime possibility is that the profit motive of everyone is almost completely maximized. That is why this strategy keeps me up at night. First, for the lobbyists it is subtle. It isn't a bill that says, "We can't compete with Keith, so we are taking away his business," but it would have that effect. Second, for the politicians it is subtle. It raises the cost of self-insurance, but they can hide behind statistics—that the large insurers will be more than happy to cook up. Third, this is because, the large insurers would also look to profit from the additional businesses that could no longer self-insure. And they would go back as well to business as usual and the magic "discounts" that they also profit from.

Fortunately, now that the state of Oklahoma is in, and probably wouldn't be effected by a bill raising the minimum amount of re-insurance, even the cronies' best strategy will likely only slow down the progress of a free market-based, transparent, high-quality health care movement.

Health Care for All

Health care isn't a right, but it is a necessity. To speak economically for a second, health care is a fairly inelastic good. That means that as the price increases the demand for that good isn't expected to change much. For instance, if you need a cast, the cost of the cast isn't likely to change your demand.

This inelasticity is the argument that the left uses to "prove" that a single-payer system is needed. Their argument is that if a hospital, insurance company, or doctor can charge anything for care, then they will. The problem is that economies don't work that way. Once a price gets too high, some entrepreneur will see an opportunity (the profit motive will reach a threshold level) to enter the market, and they will come in and compete. Therefore, the runaway price argument just isn't true.

In fact, if we look at recent examples where prices in health care have run away, it isn't because of free markets: it is because of government intervention in those markets. It is about a lack of understanding about how business work—the Profit Motive—that causes the problems each time. The case of Turing Pharmaceuticals is a prime example. They raised the price of Daraprim from $13.50/pill to $750. But like the hospitals we discussed earlier, the actions of Turing are the symptom. The underlying issue, or disease, is that the government has manipulated the market and ignored the Profit Motive and the results of that motivation in relation to those regulations.

What Turing did was appalling, but the government had created a market in which it was almost impossible to stop the price increase. For a competitor to bring a drug to market they needed to pass the FDA's approval process, which at the time was longer than ten months. That means that if "Acme Inc." wanted to introduce their own Daraprim, the drug was off-patent, so they would need to announce their intentions, pay for a ten-month review process, and only then could they compete. At that point, Turing pharmaceuticals could easily lower their price to even lower than what "Acme Inc." could afford since they had just paid for a ten-month review process while Turing would have been earning more than $700/pill that was more than the a normal market would bear. To fix the problem—the government's solution—was an expedited review process. Now a Daraprim competitor can be approved in six months, the government's version of a four-minute mile.

The government is the barrier to letting markets function because Turing pharmaceuticals was acting rationally—evil but rational—when they raised the price of their drug. The right solution is to inspect what government rule was Turing leveraging to take advantage of the broken market and to attempt to fix that provision. The solution is pretty simple: Give companies instant access to the market. That means that instead of Daraprim being able to overcharge customers for ten months, they could be undercut in minutes. That is enough incentive for a company to keep their prices in check.

Further, as we have already pointed out, hospitals are doing the same thing that Turing pharmaceuticals did by raising prices a multiple beyond what a functioning market would allow because of the rules protecting their businesses. Nonprofit hospitals, higher subsidies, higher payments from the government for the same procedure, anticompetitive employment practices, and every other tool at their disposal is to limit competition. Those should all be considered, in my mind, business as usual given Profit Motive. It isn't that the hospitals are doing wrong—they are just trying to kill their competition. That problem is the government is allowing itself to be used as a part of their strategy.

Again, given Profit Motive, the actions of hospitals are exactly what we would expect any functioning business to do, but the government should get out of the way, and in places where the government is determined to be involved, they should at least limit their involvement to the least amount possible.

Okay, so the government is a bad player when the market is bifurcated, public and private, but many would say that is all the more reason to fully transform the system into a single payer health-care system. Theoretically, assuming that no individuals are actually involved, this is a great idea. The problem is that people are involved, Profit Motives are involved, and, most importantly, our health is involved.

Doctors don't want to go to school for years, take on the liability, shoulder the pressure, and work the hours not to make a profit. Government bureaucrats will be under pressure to cut costs, and that means that all of the administration won't be working for the interest of the patient, but instead they will likely be working for their next paycheck. Following the individual incentives of anyone in a single-payer system will lead to the conclusion that the patient-physician relationship is one of the last things on anyone's list.

Therefore, the forecast for a single-payer system is fairly bleak: low research and development, decreased competition, decreased access, and decreased quality.

Fortunately, we don't have to look too far to prove this right. One of the few real scientific studies done on health care in the

United States was done on an expansion of the Medicaid population in Oregon. It is hard to do scientific studies in health care because randomization is unethical in many of the circumstances. However, when Oregon decided to open up their Medicaid roles, they decided to do it with a lottery. A randomized experiment had begun, and the end result is that the people on Medicaid were no better off than the people without.

The problem for the people who were "lucky" enough to win the lottery and were put on Medicaid was that they still needed to find care. Because of low pay, high liability, and high staff time involved with Medicaid patients, there isn't much incentive for doctors or hospitals to see them. So they limit the amount of these patients that they see.

You might say, "Well if they could only see Medicaid patients, they would see them!" People experiencing wait times in places where they have tried similar things would disagree. In Canada, for a long time, there were more CAT scan machines available in veterinarian offices than were available in the entire health-care system. Lines were so long that they had doctors in charge of the lines to make the call on who was a priority. To be sure, many people in these lines became sicker because of them. Others flew to Oklahoma to escape the oppressive "Health care for all!" schemes they were in.

The right way to provide health care to everyone is to get out of the way and let Profit Motives rule. Health care is a great market. It is one of the perfect goods that demand will always be there, and demand for health care will almost always be at the top of everyone's list of things that they need to buy. A billionaire can only eat so many pancakes, but they can have almost unlimited demand for health care. That means that the market is perfect for entrepreneurship—innovation—and competition and generations of entrepreneurs to join the fight.

When entrepreneurs fight, it means that quality is getting better and/or price is coming down. This is should result in profit-driven health care for all.

PROFIT MAN

Given the choice between two doctors—Dr. Profit Man and Dr. "Free"—you should always choose Dr. Profit Man.

Dr. "Free" is never actually free. How would he survive on nothing? So unless you are receiving charity-care, you are going to pay for "Free" somehow. You are going to wait in line, you might overpay in insurance every month, or if the government is funding the "Free" service, you might just be lining the pockets of the politicians and their friends. If you are visiting Dr. "Free," he isn't looking at you like a patient; he isn't looking at you like a client. He is looking at you like a profit center. The more he can bill for seeing you without actually doing anything for you, the more money Dr. "Free" can make. After all you aren't paying. Why would you care how much that it costs?

The longer you live, the more money Dr. Profit Man makes. He makes money when you bring in others; he makes money because you like his service, and you keep coming. Dr. Profit Man views you as a patient and a client. He wants you to be happy. The waiting room becomes a reception. The visit becomes an experience. Visiting Dr. Profit Man is an amazing thing that you want to tell your friends about, and Dr. Profit Man wants you to tell your friends.

Whenever someone talks about wanting to go see Dr. "Free" they should be warned.

6

The For-Profit Nonprofit

"BUT I RUN A 'NON' PROFIT," a colleague stressed to me while attempting to prove why his organization was better than another for-profit organization by displaying his altruistic motivations. However, that claim is normally the opposite of "altruistic," and in fact most of the time that people use the term "altruism" it is smart to be skeptical of their motivations. This is because they are hiding their Profit Motives.

Nonprofits are supposed to work toward the betterment of the community. That's why the government gives them a special, tax-exempt advantage. However, after watching the inner workings of nonprofits closely for more than ten years, it is clear to me that that most of the time this special advantage does a disservice to the people who are being served and to the donors and even the generic taxpayer that needs to make up for the lost revenue. One of the biggest problems with nonprofits is the perverse Profit Motive. Payers are not the clients, at least not in a normal sense.

Normally, if you walk into a store and pay for a Snickers bar, you get a Snickers bar. You won't pay more than that Snickers is worth to you, and the store won't sell it to you for less than they think it is worth to you. However, a nonprofit doesn't function in the same way. Money comes in from donors, but the Snickers (goods and/or services) usually go to someone else at a separate time. Donors are usually willing to give more than the Snickers is worth, and recipients are willing to accept much less than a Snickers bar is worth because they didn't pay for the candy. Almost every motivation is set up in a way to either waste money or short the recipients.

In the case of an organization like the Red Cross, every single executive who draws a salary from them means that fewer families will go without food donations from this charity during the next emergency. In the case of think tanks, it means that people who are the consumers of their work and services aren't the ones who paid for it, which is also a problem in almost all nonprofits. In the case of churches, it means that instead of serving the CEO Upstairs, the head of the church must necessarily also focus on the donors and staff, and that affects a church's culture.

It is not bad that each of these different organizations have a Profit Motive, but what is bad, and can be harmful, is when they attempt to deny that the motivations exist.

When a nonprofit fails to recognize that profit drives people, they are unlikely to be successful. Just like any business, employees need motivation. Are the employees at a church there to serve their religion? Yes, but they are also there to pay their mortgage, work their mind, and help build a business, or spread their religion. If a nonprofit leader doesn't provide these possibilities to staff, then they will likely lose staff members. Additionally, if a nonprofit fails to recognize Profit Motive, their donors will probably fail to see the benefit (their profit) of donating, and the nonprofit will quickly wither and cease to exist.

While it may feel altruistic to only care about an organization's mission, it's kind of like running a store and not caring about what any of the paying customers are asking for. Nonprofits often fail because their leaders don't recognize that their donors might want something different from what the people they are trying serve want. In other words, they fail because they are trying to be altruistic. Profit is good, but for many in the nonprofit space, it can be hard to fully accept.

One example in the world of political advocacy is that the most effective public policy campaign is often done by spending time inside the halls of Congress educating staff. However, donors can't see that educational process, and instead they are often sold by the creation of big billboards or advertisement campaigns that they can see. The best think tank development staff (donor sales-people) know to build the price of the effective campaign into the ask for the advertising campaign, but if they want to bring the donor onboard they often have to lead with the big-visible project.

The end result is an inefficient business that wastes resources on actions that aren't as productive as they could be in order to secure more funding to accomplish the goal that they are ineffectually attempting to attain.

The Profit Motive of nonprofits exists, and because of the way that motivation works, the whole market is an interesting one to explore. The donor is the buyer, and the people being served are the products.

Religion and Church

I wasn't raised in an uber-religious family, but as a good Midwestern family we went to church almost every Sunday (unless of course the Royals were playing and the weather was nice). That meant that I was close enough to the eye of the storm that I didn't really see many of the interesting incentives of the church until I reached college. But, once in college, my eyes were opened. It was almost amusing, but it involves the belief systems of people that I take very seriously.

I went to William Jewell. It is a small Baptist College in Liberty, Missouri, with about the same number of students that were at my high school. It was small, but it was known for strong academics, and I flourished—well I survived, which is more that I probably would have done at a larger school. While at William Jewell I had an average of three New Testaments given to me each year. I can only imagine that the people who gave them to me—by sliding them under my dorm room door—benefited by feeling that they were trying to convert me, but the only real person that was benefiting from this was the company that had printed New Testaments that were small enough to be slid under doors—pure genius.

Outside of college I have seen the same pushes from individuals on occasion, but in general it seems to be more of an organizational push that drives religion and churches. The thing about churches, religions, and religious colleges is that they benefit from gaining believers. They benefit as missionaries, they benefit by growing their community, but they also–or at least hope to—benefit financially. Stories about religions, or people affiliated with a religion, trying to profit financially are even in the Bible:

> And Jesus entered into the temple of God, and cast out all them that sold and bought in the temple, and overthrew the tables of the money-changers, and the seats of them that sold the doves.
>
> —Matthew 21:12

Of course in that story Jesus gets mad at the profiteers, but that hasn't stopped other religions and some Christians from trying to profit at the expense of the their parishioners. At the beginning of the book I mentioned the Profit Motive that a church has, or the head of the church has, in maintaining the old rites of a given religion. That is true, but now that we are into this a bit more, I want to take it further.

There is almost always going to also be pressure to liberalize religious belief systems. It can be hard to be told that lusting after wealth—being motivated by profit—is bad. New religions have always popped up, but in recent years it seems to be an even larger trend than in the past and for religious leaders to be motivated to make money.

The thing about religion that we touched on earlier, is that it is a ripe place for a huckster, a charlatan, to come in and sell. For instance, Catholicism is hard to follow. Did you know that there were rules about when you can put up Christmas lights? Did you know that there are rules, or traditions, in Catholicism that also dictate when you need to take your Christmas lights down? And, if you don't, your house will be haunted by a demon, one for each decoration not put away, for the whole next year. That is a religion with really strict rules! Another tough thing about Catholicism is that it doesn't really give all of the answers.

There is no point in the practice of Catholicism at which someone is going to hand you a map that lets you know the life path to take to make it to heaven. The same problems can be widely applied to the rules of other primary religions or religious sects.

However, some of the newer religions, or one-off churches, saw the market gap that this ambiguity caused and have jumped on this opportunity. Nondenominational mega churches have shot up across the country, not preaching any theology in particular, but attempting to make having a religious faith easier. The people filling in this market gap could be good people. They could themselves be very religious; they could merely oppose hypocrisy that they see in some religions, and every bone in their body might be well-intentioned. But between the perverse profit motives that are created by the nonprofit status of a church, and the perverse business incentives that a "belief"-based organization can have, this would be the perfect place for someone who is not a believer to jump in and take advantage of good people.

What would a church that a con man starts look like? The answer is probably something similar to what the modern mega churches look like now. They would have very well-produced propaganda, they would be more liberal than more established religions, and they would be more focused on the business and growth aspects than the older, stodgier religions.

The "belief" aspect of a religion, gives the con artist an advantage that he doesn't have when selling snake oil to cure ailments. In a religion, they can just say that what product or advice they offer must not work because the user doesn't believe enough—and therefore entice a person to buy the equivalent of even more fetid oil, so that they can be allowed to prove their belief.

But "belief" factor isn't the only power the con artist has when running a religion. There is also the power that our government hands to churches and is what I'm focusing on in this chapter: the fact that churches are nonprofits. If the government didn't award them this title, they would be looked at differently.

A for-profit church would be explicit about at least part of its motivations to exist. This might not stop a charlatan, but they wouldn't be able to completely hide under a veil of charity. The sales pitch from the pulpit under a for-profit regime changes to an argument more like: "If you want our church to stay alive, we need you to donate to $X dollars, and that money is going to go to these certain projects" instead of saying: "You should give us 10 percent of your income if you are a true believer." The relationship becomes more of a win-win, a true capitalist transaction, and hopefully a trap for the con artist who is no longer able to rip off the taxpayer and his parishioners. This person could then only sell to his or her parishioners.

I also want to clarify that I do not think all churches are bad. It is just a fact that a church can do better by profiting from "belief," and therefore it is something to be fully aware of in your surroundings. A book will never be able to answer questions about your religion for you, but if you question the profit motive of specific teachings or activities of your church, you might be able to identify trouble within in your church, and you might then also be able to help your church out.

"As a pastor, I've seen many congregations and other clergy who are uncomfortable talking about money within their community. Giving can be a delicate subject and is often regarded as a personal and private matter, yet how churches and organizations steward their resources is best approached with accountability and transparency.

I believe that financial giving should be a prayerful decision for participants. I also believe that money is a tool that allows us to further our mission, share God's love with more people, and effect positive change in our communities. Money allows us to purchase music for worship services that might bring healing or encouragement. Money enables us to buy books for our volunteers to read at after-school programs. Money gives us the opportunity to build buildings for ministry, to run medical clinics, to feed the hungry, to do the work that Jesus taught us to do.

Part of what it means to be the church is to invite people to give, of themselves and their resources, so that together we would answer the call to make disciples of Jesus Christ for the transformation of the world."

—Rev. Molly Simpson, United Methodist clergy
From an interview I held with her on January 17, 2017

In fact, if a good church recognizes profit motive the members leading the organization might start looking at the business practices of the more successful churches. They might consider the following questions: Should they raise the production value of their sermon? Should they increase the production value of their recruiting material? For instance, offering high school Bible studies might help to engage younger people, but depending on the time being put into offering the classes might not be the best investment for the church. High school students are likely to disappear for college, and the chances that they will live in the same place after college are merely a guess. Additionally, if they are going to the church it is likely their parents are already attending—

and hopefully giving. On the other hand, a Bible study for young professionals might be an amazing investment. When engaging the young professionals in a community, they might not at first be able to give high dollar amounts, but their income will likely increase as will the size of their family (inside sales are easier than outside sales).

If you assume that your church, any church, has to act in a profit motivated way (whatever that profit is), decisions can be made with a purpose that helps everyone out, including deciding whether or not that church is right for you.

Motivations: Profit vs. Nonprofit

Admitting that donors and the people served might have different needs is important, but when a nonprofit denies that a profit motive might even exist, the organization can be harmful. The colleague I referred to at the beginning of this chapter runs a nonprofit that serves a certain community of entrepreneurs. But many of the people involved in the organization's leadership feed like hungry vampires off of the entrepreneurs they serve. It isn't so much a nonprofit that they run as an organization used as a trap to lure future customers. This obviously isn't very altruistic. On the other hand, another colleague runs a for-profit that serves the same community of entrepreneurs, and the leaders are up-front about their profit and attract entrepreneurs who understand that motivation.

Which business model is better for the people that they claim to serve? The for-profit one, of course. It provides a lot more value, and the value provided is win-win, which allows the for-profit company (and gives them an even bigger incentive) to work with more inventors in the future. On the other hand, nonprofits that rely on donations have a slightly different motivation. In fact, the only way that staff can financially profit at the nonprofit is if the organization serves fewer of the very people their mission says they serve. The incentives are flipped. Furthermore, denial of profit motive forces nonprofit leaders to hide the reasoning behind what they are doing. This can express itself in lots of ways, but it is almost always harmful to the people they serve.

Given the reverse incentives, the ability to fake altruism, and the government provided competitive advantage (not paying taxes) it would seem reasonable to conclude that I'm saying nonprofits are a bad thing. They aren't.

Some organizations should be nonprofits. Others—many others—shouldn't be. However, given that it is legal to create nonprofits for organizations that probably should be for-profit, the best advice is to be vigilant. When you pay attention to Profit Motive, meaning when you pay attention to the incentives that drive a charity, you can maximize your own charity, and you are better prepared to protect yourself against false help. You might even be able to identify how to run your own charity and might be able to identify gaps in the market that you didn't know existed.

The Profit-Driven Effects of Charitable Tax Breaks

The nonprofit example that I am closest to is the politically infamous "think tank." These organizations are staffed with policy experts, academics, outreach staff, communications staff, and, most importantly, development staff (referenced above as the donor sales people).

There are lots of different versions of nonprofits, but the most common kind to discuss, and the one that we will talk about most here, is a called a 501(c)(3) by the IRS. This tax designation covers "charities," and donations to a c3 are tax deductible. The tax benefit gives these organizations a real advantage over organizations without the tax benefit.

However, the tax benefit also causes these charities to seek out funding from a certain group of people that they might not have without the tax incentive: rich people. The more money that some-one makes, the higher the taxes they pay. Because of the charitable tax deduction, the rich can give 20 percent to 30 percent more without feeling any difference in their bank accounts. Somebody that isn't as well off will only see a benefit of 10 percent–15 percent. Rich people have more money, so they are a good market for donations anyway, but the charitable deduction makes them even more attractive to a charity development staff than making trans-actions under a normal free market absent government intrusion.

Tax law is definitely important in how nonprofits are shaped as far as what they do and how they spend their money, but there's more to this. Attempting to look further into nonprofits to get a better understanding about why donors give money in the first place, in other words, their Profit Motive, is a must. Despite the way that many talk about donations as "necessary to get a tax break," a donation still costs money, and as we just pointed out, the donations just feel like they are discounted money (less expen-sive). So, what is the "Profit Motive" of donors?

Nonprofit donors are the back bone that our charity system rides on. Without the "goes-into: there is no "goes-out" to provide the resources to the people they are trying to serve.

So donors are necessary to finance a charity. That means that they need to be found and developed. And one of the major rev-elations that solidified my understanding that "profit" drives the world is when I finally understood that donors are sold the way that everyone is sold.

Donors want "profit" like anyone that is transacting some-thing. Uri Gneezy and John List mention this in their book, *The Why Axis*, when they state:

> Most people would say they give because they want to help others. But is such altruism the only reason for peo-ple's generosity? Our research reveals it is not. In fact,

> our multiple field experiments with several different char-
> itable causes—which involved communications with over
> a million people—show compelling evidence that (brace
> yourself) our psychological reasons for donating are often
> more selfish than most of us would care to admit.[31]

The fact that a donation is like any other transaction is important and really proves how these baseline motivations help drive
much of the world around us.

Another important factor to note (like in other areas such as
work, business growth, and home) is that not everyone is looking for the most *monetary* profit. Some donors are looking for
other things. Some donors want to help, some donors want to
have influence, and there is even one class of donor that actually
"needs" to give money away.

Many foundations have rules that force them to give away a
certain percentage of the foundation's money every year. The sales
pitch to this kind of group is very different from a pitch to a first-
time donor spending their own money.

Development professionals figure out what the donor wants
as "profit" and attempts to figure out if that is possible to provide.

People who have money to give usually made their money
through hard work and effective use of their resources along the
way. These types of people aren't likely to just throw their money
away. Donors need to be sold.

Big Donors and Good Nonprofits

You might be ready to conclude that I don't like nonprofits, but I
only don't like bad ones. And since the incentives are all wrong
at nonprofits, the good ones are few and far between. There is not
much that can be done about that except patience and due diligence.

Whether you are donating a few hundred dollars, a few thousand dollars, or a few million dollars, finding a worthy nonprofit

is hard. However, as your donations start edging upwards—and definitely by the time that you are donating millions of dollars—you can start adding to your odds by leveraging profit motives as well as increasing your due diligence, your oversight, and your overall involvement.

I don't personally know a lot of large dollar donors, and that includes T. Boone Pickens. But when it comes to Mr. Pickens, I know people that he has invested in, and I know people that he has hired to vet organizations for his philanthropy work. Because of what I know about the people with whom he surrounds himself, the organizations that he has invested in, the people that he has chosen to invest in, and the difference that he made with his philanthropy—I like him. He describes his strategies this way:

> We're participatory, interested, involved, and proactive. We know where we want to make a difference. We find people that have the leadership skills and the capability to make a difference, and we fund them. We're always looking for leadership. We like results and want to ensure that the individuals, entities, and organizations we support are doing what they said they were going to do. When we find someone who is doing a good job, we consider them a client of ours instead of us being a client of theirs.
>
> —T. Boone Pickens
> *The First Billion Is the Hardest:*
> *Reflections on a Life of Comebacks and America's Energy Future*

What sets the people and groups that he is working with apart from the rest is the fact that they have strong leadership skills. In the investor world, there is actually a phrase for this style or idea. It is called investing in the jockey instead of the horse.

The thing about large-dollar donors is that by picking the right people working on the right project, they can reverse the normal nonprofit donor/client relationship. Instead of working with a development professional who is motivated to bring in money because of a commission, and instead of being sold a short-run exciting thing to donate to, the big donor can work with the leadership of an organization to really help drive them toward their long-run goal. They can bypass the short-run profit motives of the individuals of the project and help the leaders move toward the future.

In the for-profit business world, investors help drive a company to the next level. In the for-profit world, these changes are driven in several ways: Investors might invest in tranches that can only be reached by hitting certain milestones, investors might introduce the leaders of the company they are invested in to good potential partners, and they might even help in the planning. But individual clients for a for-profit don't have that kind of input. The examples of how donors can contribute to an organization are the same in the nonprofits, but in nonprofits it isn't clients or investors, it is just small-dollar donors and large-dollar donors.

Each nonprofit has different levels for when they might consider someone a large-dollar donor. But with his overall donations to organizations totaling close to $2 billion dollars there is no question that T. Boone Pickens is a large donor. I think that it is important to talk about Mr. Pickens and his charitable investments because he is truly approaching his giving the way that he approached business, and his results have been just as impressive. As he says in *The First Billion Is the Hardest*, "At my age, a dollar saved is a dollar wasted. I decided I didn't want to wait until after I was dead to give away my fortune; I wanted to see the impact of my donations in my lifetime." And, importantly to get the most out of his donations he uses an approach that take the normal perverse incentives of the Profit Motives of nonprofits out of the equation.

To accomplish his goals, he has had to be aggressive, insightful, and ambitious. The results that he has seen are not just from good luck. To accomplish this, Mr. Pickens has had to engage each group, and he has had to pick the right people. And he has used his money to leverage the profit motive of the organizations he has donated to and has leveraged other donors as well. The results are that everyone involved accomplished their goals of profit-making by building better, bigger, more efficient and effective organizations that serve and also educate people to have a positive effect from top to bottom.

The person that he has invested in whom I am closest to is Terry Neese. Terry has done a lot of things, but as mentioned earlier, her work with women entrepreneurs in Afghanistan and Rwanda is one of the most effective that I have ever seen. And after reading more about the philosophy and goals that Mr. Pickens brings to his giving, this investment makes even more sense. Terry Neese is a leader, she is running a novel program, and every dollar spent will have lasting effects.

Terry's Peace Through Business program isn't extravagant, but she has costs. She needs an administrative office to help direct traffic for the program and she needs staff to teach in the different countries. She also needs to print some marketing materials, and she needs a marketing/development budget large enough to help grow the organization. If instead of teaching entrepreneurship Terry was just give away T-shirts, the investment in handing out those T-shirts would only get a one-time return on investment. However, Terry's organization is teaching people a skill. The people that she is teaching are hiring people. The people they are hiring are supporting others. And, the staff that she has hired are getting even better at what they do. The investment in Terry and Terry's organization is getting three or four times the return. It isn't financial profit, but a return with a multiplier this large is the type of return that an investor would look for, and in his charitable investments this is the type of return that Mr. Pickens tends to get. Mr. Pickens' investment in Terry's organization wasn't a fluke. The successes that her organization have had are typical of successes that Mr. Pickens had in the business world, and he is now doing the same in the philanthropic world.

Because I was working on this book I was given access to some of the people that Mr. Pickens has invested in. I was interested because of the big-dollar donor relationship. I had read about his charity and had followed his pledge to give away extreme amounts of money on TV, but I wanted to understand what types of groups—and people—he was investing in.

One of those philanthropic investments was with the Junior League of Dallas, where he funded a leadership development program. This wasn't one of his biggest grants; it was around $250,000, but the organization didn't need a lot of capital. They just wanted to start a new program. And now that program continues with funding from others who also recognize its benefit. Because of the initial grant from Mr. Pickens, the program has nearly 250 alum and has helped to increase the positive effect of the community service contributions by the Junior League in Dallas.

The Junior League is a great organization and is recognized as one of the foremost training organizations for women to serve the community.

Over the past 95 years, the Junior League of Dallas (JLD) has transformed the region by cultivating leaders to address the critical needs of our community. The impact of the trained volunteer force of more than 5,000 women is significant. Each year, JLD members give more than 130,000 hours of uncompensated volunteer service, which is even more impressive given that over 70 percent of the membership works outside the home. The dollar value of the uncompensated hours equates to nearly $2

million, which combined with the $1 million dollars in fund-
ing awarded to community agencies, provides $3 million
of support to the community. This means that each dollar
donated to the JLD results in triple the value.

—Christina Norris
Former President Junior League of Dallas

In 2008 the Dallas Junior League reached out to former leaders of the organization, and according to their responses their
leaders served on 90 boards and had raised $150 million for the
Dallas community. Mr. Pickens wasn't just putting his money
toward one-time handouts when he awarded the Junior League
of Dallas with a grant; he was investing in current leaders in a
way that would help create future leaders. His profit motive, and
theirs, wasn't just hosting a class. It was to have a dramatic effect
on the community.

Choosing the Dallas Junior League wasn't just a coincidence.
While small-dollar donors should look to invest their money into
charities that provide a high return like Junior Leagues, they can
usually only attempt to pick the best charities when donating to
a cause. Mr. Pickens goes a bit further, though. He has a team
and built his charity organization like a business. In fact, when
he started his foundation it was the most money that he had ever
started a business with. One of his assets, and one of my friends, is
Marti Carlin. Mr. Pickens writes about Marti in *The First Billion Is
the Hardest* and calls her his "Bird Dog." It is Marti's job to find the
leaders. She sorts through the hundreds and thousands of proposals,
she talks to people, and she is the one that Mr. Pickens relies on to
sort through the mass of literature they receive. Marti does the vetting to make sure that the foundation is only working with the best.

The job of Marti is to pick the right people, and then her job
is make sure that the organizations are getting the most out of the

funding that they can and should. Just throwing money at something is not a very effective means to success. That is when treating the recipients of their charitable donations as clients comes into play. Mr. Pickens wants to make sure that these clients are getting their money's worth. When a big-dollar donor engages in this process in an effective manner, this can change the normal nonprofit organization's relationship with its donors from merely regarding them simply as a donor to treating donors as a business partner or even as an investor. The can truly help the organization grow and thrive.

Godwin G. Dixon explains how Mr. Pickens contributed greatly to community service organizations in Dallas:

> Mr. Pickens has always thoroughly vetted organizations before donating to ensure that he will get a good return on his investments, and that is how he looks at them— as investments. He invests in people, organizations and causes that he believes are making and will continue to make a difference in society. We all know of the investments he made in Oklahoma State University's football team which turned a historically under-performing program into a perennial top 25 team. What does not get as much press is his significant investments in OSU's academic programs that have had, and will continue to have a material impact on countless students. His investments in Texas Women's University, Baylor Cancer Hospital, UTSW and MD Anderson have and will continue to significantly advance research and development in the area of health for years to come.
>
> Mr. Pickens made the lead gift of $18.4 M for the Dallas T. Boone Pickens Hospice and Palliative Care Center, and his $2M gift completed the $17M renovation campaign at Grace Presbyterian Village, a continuing care retirement community in Southeast Oak Cliff neighborhood in Dallas.

In both cases, Mr. Pickens' investments not only help the immediate needs of families, but have broader goals of helping the community as well as providing examples of effective programs that can be duplicated around the country. For instance, his investment in the Palliative Care Center will help reduce suffering and lower the cost of end of life care for families around Dallas. The average costs at end of life in Dallas are more than 10 percent higher than national mediums in Dallas and through Mr. Pickens investment, that will now be addressed. In addition to offering better outcomes for patients and families it will also be a great addition to the palliative care curriculums for area educational institutions. The students who do rotations through this center will have a much greater understanding of best practices in end of life care and be better able to serve not just our local community but communities throughout the country as they move on after graduation.

—Godwin G. Dixon, Executive Vice Chairman
Presbyterian Communities and Services Board of Directors;
President and CEO Presbyterian Communities
and Services Foundation
From my interview with him on December 20, 2016

Once involved with organizations, Marti continues to work hard to ensue their success. I have watched her at events. Marti doesn't attend nonprofit fundraisers because she enjoys dry chicken or hotel ballroom décor. Marti attends events to work. Not only does she want to make sure that everything that should go into a big event has gone into it, she also wants to help get others involved with the charity. T. Boone Pickens is competitive—and his team exemplifies this.

The way that the Pickens Foundation is run, and the value that they get out of their investments, is what leveraging profit motive is all about. They aren't attempting to maximize the size of their donations. They aren't attempting to maximize their media. The foundation, and everyone who works for it (outside of their own motivations), is on board with attempting to get the biggest return possible on every charitable investment they make. And, from knowing Marti, I would assume that Mr. Pickens hired the members of his team because their personal motivations are aligned with his.

The Center for BrainHealth in Dallas, another charitable investment of Mr. Picken's, has a wonderful educational program described by its director, Sara Bond:

According to Washington Center researchers, increasing U.S. ed ucational achievement so that the average American score matched the O.E.C.D. average would add 1.7 percent to the nation's gross domestic product and tax revenues would increase by a $902 billion over the next 35 years.

We at the Center for BrainHealth, part of The University of Texas at Dallas, are transforming and inspiring curious classroom learners through innovative thinking training. Our scientifically-validated program has grown exponentially since 2006, reaching more than 50,000 middle school students across the country. Positive results are striking. With training, students across the socioeconomic spectrum exhibit more than a 25 percent increase in abstract reasoning, 18 percent increase in new learning, and dramatically improved graduation rates. We are training future innovators—an investment in human capital.

—Sandra Bond Chapman, PhD
Founder and Chief Director, Center for BrainHealth
From my interview with her on December 20, 2016

These relationships of charities and their donors become a huge win-win when Mr. Pickens contributes to them. For the charity, they get a big donor that is engaged and invested in seeing their money pay dividends. On the other hand, the donor can cut through the usual sales pitch and turn into a partner instead of being a client.

Mr. Pickens and his team were able to see the 3-to-1 ratio that Christina Norris mentioned for the Junior League of Dallas also provide the capstone on a project at Grace Presbyterian Village and therefore realize the multiple there, and his funding and support of the Center for BrainHealth might even be increasing the GDP of the whole country.

So, just looking at three of his investments in Dallas: the Junior League, Grace Presbyterian, and The Center for Brain-Health we see that the three projects are all what Mr. Pickens surely thought of as "investment multipliers." And, these three are just a sample of his foundation's portfolio. I am told this list of valuable, multiplier style of donations could go on and on.

But what did it provide Mr. Pickens? What was his motive?

In Mr. Pickens' book *The First Billion Is the Hardest* he includes what he calls "Booneisms." These little insights are scattered throughout, but one of them actually helps to provide the answer here. Number 21 is "I love making money, but I also love giving it away. Not as much as making it, but it's a very close second." Mr. Pickens likes giving away money. He earned it; he can do what he wants with his money. As I said earlier, he is also competitive. If Mr. Pickens didn't enjoy giving money away, he would still be competitive, and that would produce some profit-motive-driven symptoms that include giving away money. When Mr. Pickens is given an award, it is usually at an event that also includes a fundraiser. Mr. Pickens loves setting records at these fundraisers. That means that the charity gets more money, they have a higher goal to beat next time, and it also means that he wins.

However, even in this the fact that Mr. Pickens made a lot of money, the fact that he likes giving it away, and the fact that he is also competitive provides a multiplier to what he is going to accomplish—even when he is without the team that he uses to increase the value of his donations.

Looking for answers to what drives big donors is hard. The main issue is that they aren't everywhere. There just aren't that many people who have been as successful as T. Boone Pickens. And, most of the time when you find them, their backgrounds, ages, and motivations are all so different that it would be hard to generalize. But what should be easy to understand is that getting funding from a large donor isn't as easy as McDonald's selling customers on Super-Sizing their value meals. In fact, working with a large donor often isn't about selling at all. However, if you are a leader and you are working on a project that you love and believe in, and that project might be able to be scaled, whether you are pitching Mr. Pickens or someone else, it is important to pay attention to what they want.

They Are Only an Organization

Nonprofits are really just for-profits under a different tax regime. The methods for each of the business models to run successfully are the same. Products need to identified, customers/clients/payers need to be identified, and the way that the organization is different needs to be identified. When I advise startups, inventors, or nonprofits the advice is almost the same.

The reason is that the profit motive of the customers is always the same. They want something for their money. No matter how much an entrepreneur would like to think that their invention, business, or cause is so good that everyone will come flocking to it, this just isn't the case. People need to be convinced to give up their money.

So if you are running a nonprofit, you should try to think of yourself as a for-profit every once in a while. Maybe it isn't smart—given the restrictions of the tax code—to always think about a nonprofit that you run as a for-profit, but putting on your for-profit thinking cap can be very useful. You can make sure that you aren't misleading your current givers. That isn't good for long-term profits. If you are trying to think like a for-profit you can also make sure that you are staying current. And, in some cases where it might not be good to change with market or social trends—religions are a good example—you might be able to identify areas where staying current isn't helpful and where it is. Just identifying these important parts of your business/nonprofit can help market yourself better to possible members.

Also, your for-profit hat might help you see the areas that provide a bigger bang for your buck. Thinking like this can help pull in big donors and also increase the effectiveness of your organization.

The same thing goes for prospective donors. Instead of looking at a charity as a nonprofit, looking at the nonprofit as a for-profit that you are investing in can aid in making better and more effective Pickens-like choices. Is a nonprofit just throwing away money? Are they doing things that have no benefit to the long-run growth of the organization or fulfillment of the organization? Or is the organization that you are looking at investing in being run by a leader that understands the mission, how to achieve it effectively, and making the right decisions to accomplish this?

Additionally, many entrepreneurs start off with ideas that they should be using for starting for-profit organizations, and are not asking themselves the right questions outlined here. When they do get around to asking the right questions, they will often see that their client and the payer are two different groups. That often means that a nonprofit, or donor model is the best. As a business owner there are many drawbacks to starting a nonprofit instead of a for-profit business, but if this is the right business model for you, then you could be fighting against a wrong-headed choice for the rest of the life of the business.

While there are some net benefits to nonprofits, including sometimes being a more apt business model, the primary reason I am not a large fan of nonprofits is that being a nonprofit gives organizations a sense of a government endorsement, and too few donors look at them correctly because of this tacit endorsement. Always think about the profit motive of any nonprofit before participating in an event, donating to an event, or even starting your own.

PROFIT MAN

A nonprofit? That isn't something that Profit Man is interested in. However, given the government tax break, a government-provided advantage over his competitors, Profit Man might make an exception.

If Profit Man was running a nonprofit, he would run it almost exactly like a normal business. He would consider supply, demand, pricing, sales, marketing, branding, and mission. Profit Man would understand that his donors are not the ones receiving the benefit from his group's work and would figure out how to ensure that they were receiving value for their donation.

Profit Man might get rich running his nonprofit, but like a for-profit organization his greed would necessarily need to stay in check. Unlike a nonprofit organization, if Profit Man decided to be greedy, donors would actually be aware of how much he is getting paid. For the true Profit Man, the public nature of his pay would help to keep him in check, but others that aren't truly building wealth or long-run profit often fall prey to the entice-ment of just taking more and more.

Profit Man isn't a fan of nonprofits, but when it provides him an advantage, Profit Man can be persuaded.

7

Individual Profit Motive

The Connecticut troops will not be prevailed upon to stay longer than their term (saving those who have enlisted for the next campaign, and mostly on furlough), and such a dirty, mercenary spirit pervades the whole, that I should not be at all surprised at any disaster that may happen.

—George Washington
Letter to Joseph Reed Cambridge, 28 November, 1775

IT IS A DAUNTING TASK TO CHALLENGE the leadership of George Washington, but when I read about this letter of his in David McCullough's *1776* it struck me as odd. Of course there was a "mercenary" spirit among his troops. They had left their family to fight for the general, and they were promised pay, but there was often no money for them. The general expected them to stay to fight for their country for free.

The problem is that many of them had families, and they had farms and a life outside of the army. At the same time, life inside of the army was dangerous and injurious, and they were getting ready to encamp for a full and harsh winter with poor supplies and not even much gun powder if they had to defend themselves. In other words, the soldiers didn't see much profit in staying.

George Washington understood this, but at the particular time that he wrote this letter the general was at a particularly low point. Fortunately for the general, and all of us US citizens now, things started changing fairly rapidly after this letter. Soon after the writing of the general's letter, and a lot of troops leaving, the text of a speech by King George attacking the ideas that the soldiers were standing up for made its way to the papers in the US, and this rallied the troops. It was even one of the last acts that led to the writing of the Declaration of Independence.

If the soldier had perfect knowledge of the profit that could be had for the generations of Americans that came after him, many of the soldiers might have stayed, but perfect knowledge of the future is never available. In the case of the soldiers serving in the winter of 1775 there is almost no way that they could imagine where we are now. I know that I don't blame them for leaving, and given how hard George Washington fought for pay for the soldiers, he probably wouldn't either—well, okay, he probably would still blame them. But that is one of the reasons that discussing individual profit motive is important.

It is easy to look at a business, a market, or even a movement and see that they are doing things for money. But, as we have found out from looking at profit motive in startups and some individuals in the media and politics, there are sometimes exceptions when decisions seem to be made that don't follow the commonly expected motivations. When we look at the exceptions, it is normally a variance in the profit motive of individuals that is the driver.

People need money to survive, but to increase their perceived quality of life, a person will do almost anything. Profit motive is strong in individuals, but it can be trickier to pin down. This is because everyone is different. Some people want to live in luxury, some people want to retire early, some people want more responsibility, some people want less responsibility, some people want to experience risk, and others don't, and so forth.

Personally, I enjoy and value spending time with my family and I put a high value on that. And, because of that weighting, my family has already benefitted in a lot of ways—although for several years we took a pretty good hit financially. We have now built a business that affords us a little bit of a cushion, but we had to push hard for several years when it might have been financially easier to go in a different direction in pursuit of the life we wanted.

Other people are different, though, and they pursue their profits differently. I know other people that value time with family as much as I do, but their plan is to attempt to spend more time with their family while they are still relatively young, so they are working as many hours as they can now in pursuit of their early retirement.

There are few key individual profit motive areas that I think are important to cover, so that is what I am going to focus on in this chapter. However, because of the diversity of individuals and cultures this is only a dabbling of a toe into the vast waters of the motivations of individuals.

Measuring the Importance of Money

Money isn't the primary driver of everyone, but, again, since we need money to survive, money is at least somewhere on everyone's list of motivations. And, even when money isn't at the top of somebody's list, since a business or business owner often expresses how much they value the work and effort of their employees to those employees, an individual can still use money as the guide to see if they are attaining the goals or earning the right profit.

One place where individual profit motive has had a dramatic effect is during the implementation of the Affordable Care Act. When the Affordable Care Act was passed by Democrats in Congress their goal was to provide everyone quality health care. We don't have to debate the merits of that policy goal now, but the way the Left wanted to accomplish their goal was creating a health care "exchange" where plans had to provide a certain type of coverage. To get people to enroll in an exchange plan, they employed both the use of carrots (subsidies) and sticks (fines). The goal of the

Left was to push individuals into the plans by playing with their financial incentives, or profit motive. But politics are what they are, and the Left couldn't impose a penalty big enough to really make individuals feel the pain of not enrolling. So they have consistently underperformed early forecasts.

The Left understood that they had to throttle back their "stick" because during the debate over Hillary Clinton's health-care plan in the '90s, the "stick" caused a problem because health insurance was mandated, and to enforce the rule, the penalties were necessarily draconian. Once the penalties become severe enough, a policy like this becomes effective. For instance in Finland they have income-based speeding fines, so one man just received a fine for going 65 mph in a 50 mph that cost him $103,000.[32] But fines like that seemed heavy-handed to the grassroots at that time, and Hillary started losing support for the bill.

So when the debate came up again during the Affordable Care Act, the Left had learned their lesson, and they included a low fine in the bill. I have talked with a staffer who was at the center of some of the discussions about health-care reform at the time and was told they knew the fine they were proposing was too low, but it was a risk they were willing to take. This was one of the many.

The Left understood that their plan lacked an effective "stick," but given the political realities they can be given a pass on just going with what they could. Where they shouldn't get a pass is thinking that markets were just going to do their work for them. The piece the Left wasn't prepared for was taking human incentive into account.

The bottom level of insurance and the bottom price didn't provide a high enough profit in money savings or risk abatement to warrant avoiding the fine. At least it didn't work for the younger and healthier in the population. This meant that the people that did sign up for insurance who felt that the insurance was a good deal tended to be older and, more likely, sicker than the general population.

Because the law didn't take into account that individuals would act based on their own profit motives, the law wasn't providing the coverage to the number of people that it was originally projected to cover.

The Obama Administration reacted in a similar way of being blind to motivation in an attempt to correct the situation. They begged insurance agents to help. In order to sign people up for a plan, many individuals use an insurance agent because buying insurance can be confusing and scary. But, unfortunately, under ObamaCare these agents weren't given an incentive to sign people up for ACA plans. In fact, the opposite has been the case. Insurance agents get paid by the insurance plans for signing people up. Their commission varies from person to person, but it is paid by the insurance company to the agent.

Insurance companies understand profit motive. If they have a product and they want an agent to enroll someone in that product they must be willing to pay for it. If agents don't enroll people in a certain product the insurance companies are pushing for their financial benefit, the insurance company won't want to pay much for enrollments in plans less desirable to the company. Given the mandates and regulations that the exchange plans must follow under the ACA, insurance plans are not as valuable on the exchange as others. So, what have insurance companies done? They have either stopped paying agents altogether for signing up people for an exchange plan, or they have reduced the commission to such a low rate that the commission they receive is almost a cruel joke.

For a lot of reasons, including not throwing money into a burning fire, nobody in Congress has proposed sending money to agents or forcing insurance companies to provide equal or higher commissions for enrolling individuals in exchange plans, but some profit-based ideas would help reverse (via a short-run fix, not good public policy) the problem that the legislation has had reaching the scale that the Left was hoping for.

To make matter worse, the Obama Administration understood, in part, their error and they tried fix it without additional funding but instead by writing memos that echo the sentiments of General George Washington during the winter of 1775. In an email from healthcare.gov to registered agents the Obama Administration laid out a new program to get agents to sign up more customers for exchange plans:

> Starting this month through the end of January 2017, when you help 20 or more consumers select plans through the Individual Marketplace or sign up 20 or more employers through the Small Business Health Options Program (SHOP) Marketplace, you will become a member of our HealthCare.gov Circle of Champions.

If the agent was fortunate enough to become a member of the "Circle of Champions" would he or she be showered with gifts of money? Gifts of any sort? Nope, they would then be allowed to use a badge on their website, which if effective would even further lower their bottom line and be given a piece of paper that they could hang in their office to remind themselves of this financial masochism.

The profit motive of money doesn't drive everyone, and it especially doesn't drive everyone all of the time. However, most people also aren't going to act in a way that undermines their long-run financial stability. Business owners around the world understand this principle, but it's really hard to create a public policy that relies on mandates to fully accommodate the financial motivations of people and markets, at least without draconian rules (and which also rules out the plan politically).

Entrepreneur vs. Employee

"The majority of people don't want to plan. They want to be free of the responsibility of planning. What they ask for is merely some assurance that they will be decently provided for. The rest is a day-to-day enjoyment of life."

—B.F. Skinner, *Walden Two*

What B.F. Skinner is talking about here is the difference between an entrepreneur and employee. Some people don't like planning, but one of the most important parts of this Skinner quote is his mention of "assurance." In the frame of this book, what he's referring to is that some people highly value stability, and therefore they are motivated to pursue it.

When talking with Ron Devine, one of the Owners of the BK Racing, he said, "People are structured one of two ways. They are either paycheck-oriented, or they are entrepreneurial-oriented."

Ron is an owner of a NASCAR Sprint Cup Series team, BK Racing, that has sponsors with combined annual revenues of $50 billion. The team is headquartered in Charlotte, NC, and was founded in 2012 after Ron and a few other investors acquired Red Bull Racing. In other words, Ron understands entrepreneurship.

He made his big bet on the team in 2012. He grew up around cars and racing; he used to lean out of the passenger window as he jousted at metal rings with a pool cue while being driven down a drag strip against another car doing the same in the other lane. But he left the sport (car racing not jousting) for a few years to build his company. He was successful while he was away from the sport and wanted back in. He didn't jump all in at that point and just assume a multimillion-dollar level of risk. He did his research and worked his way back into the community, including working as a part of the pit crew. Once in, he identified the true business opportunity: NASCAR advertising returns a multiple of the ad spending instead of a small percentage. For instance, if a Burger King spent $1 on advertising, the return that they expected from other markets was less than that dollar. However, every dollar spent on NASCAR advertising returns several dollars back to the business. So Ron jumped back into NASCAR. Ron takes a lot of risks, but he would say that they are smart risks.

I finished my conversation by asking him what he thinks is the most important advice that he could give entrepreneurs, and he answered, "Hire good people." I pushed him a bit, and the reasoning was fairly simple: good staff helps mitigate risk, and when things go bad they can help right the ship faster.

Ron's profit motive isn't money, although he says that his success can be measured that way. Ron's profit motive seems to be the excitement and creativity of being an entrepreneur—and doing it intelligently.

Entrepreneurs like Ron have to plan, but they will never have the assurance that Skinner spoke about some people wanting. In fact, if people have been entrepreneurs long enough, they are probably fairly confident that some of their plans won't work out as expected. Entrepreneurs seem to embrace that risk.

When I first started thinking about this difference, and the fact that almost every entrepreneur that I talked with explained the difference almost the same way, I kind of felt stuck. It would be nice and tidy for the concept of "profit motive" if it came down to "risk" as being the profit that entrepreneurs were seeking. But, while risk is exciting, and excitement, whether in business or car-jousting, could be considered profit, that seemed like a big stretch. The truth hit me, and the way that it hit me is one of the reasons that I value always looking at what others stand to gain— meaning my looking for the profit motive of others. It turns out that I was looking at the situation incorrectly, much in the way that Ron Devine describes an experience in the following story.

I'll tell you a story that brings it light. I had at one time maybe six or seven district managers that each operated somewhere between three and five units depending on the size and where they were in the pecking order. I had this brilliant idea of going to them and saying you become the franchisee, okay, and in my mind it was an incredible opportunity. So I went to some of my senior ones first, and said 'what do you think of this?' And out of six of them really only one was even remotely interested.

It was eye-opening to me, and the one that was interested was probably the one that was least qualified to do it—and he was just moderately interested in it. The other ones didn't want to take the risk of it.

Now, it was mind-boggling to me because they run the business all day every day. I guess that I kind of like steering the ship, but they were manning all the stations at the end of the day. I thought to myself, 'Why would you just not want to step up to the helm?' In a funny sort of way it's easier, but anyway it had zero traction, zero interest.

—Ron Devine, Owner BK racing
From my interview with him on December 5, 2016

I am an entrepreneur, and entrepreneurs are usually talked about as being "different" or "out there" (and those accusations about me are just from my wife), but the truth is that if we are looking at the profit motive of individuals we need to look at the individual that we are discussing. In this case we are looking at two people: a highly competent person that is a long-term employee at a company (generically) and another person that is an equally skilled entrepreneur (generically) and looking at their profit motives. When looking at that employee, it is evident that the person values security. An employee is willing to give up some autonomy because of the value they receive from having "security." On the other hand, it is obvious that the who chose to be an entrepreneur doesn't value security as highly—or if they do, they are likely seeking it the wrong way by taking on the risk of being self-employed.

The risk that an entrepreneur takes on can equal riches, or additional profit, but the riches and profit are rare, and given the increased stress that is often a part of the journey, it is unlikely that many would consider "risk" the profit motive of entrepreneurs. Financial rewards are still a part of the equation. The reward that an entrepreneur gets for foregoing a steady and promised paycheck is a time-shifted opportunity for increased long-run profits. (We call this "delayed gratification.")

Additionally, not everyone would agree with Skinner. Professional speakers, self-help gurus, and the startup celebration community often say that anybody can be an entrepreneur. But, while there can be exceptions, it definitely seems like there are two types of people: risk-takers and non-risk-takers, or in the frame of Profit Motive, people who highly value the security vs. those who don't. A non-risk-taker can be a entrepreneur, but they would need to focus on overcoming their risk aversion, and it would likely lead them down roads that might not be as good for their business as a direction they would have taken without a dislike of taking risks.

Given this piece of information, maybe we should look for people who are not risk-adverse, but not too prone to risk-taking either, and immediately fund their entrepreneurial ambitions. It turns out that it might not be that easy and introduces us at the same time to one of the opportunities and limitations that Profit Motive provides us. Profit Motive can change, and motivations can be learned.

In the book *The Why Axis* the authors Uri Gneezy and John List discuss an eye-opening "field experiment" that exposed how our society determines the way that males and women perceive risk and competition. The results of their initial studies were that men in many patriarchal cultures were more risk-prone than women by a significant amount, and women just did not like to compete as much as men do. but the researchers didn't stop there. They eventually found a matrilineal tribe, the Khasi from northeastern India, and conducted their study in this culture.

In Khasi the authors used a game in which they gave participants ten tries to throw tennis balls into a bucket for a cash reward. This experiment was based on two payment options that directly addresses the idea of profit motive as far as risk vs. security when receiving cold, hard cash is involved. The participants had the first option of earning an amount equal to one day's wages in their culture each time they landed a ball in the bucket on the ten tries. So for this first option they received money based on their successful tosses and no one else was involved. But for a second option, the participants could also compete against someone else.

If they sank more balls than their opponent on the ten tries they would receive a much higher amount of money—three times more money for each successful shot, and they could therefore receive up to a month's worth of wages. If both opponents performed equally and landed the tennis ball in the bucket the same number of times, they would both receive the lower amount of money equaling a day's wages for each successful toss. But if one had more successful tosses into the bucket than the other, the loser received no cash.

The numbers were the opposite of those found in the US or any of the other patriarchal tribe or communities that they previously had tested. The authors found that when they performed their experiment on the Khasi's, the women were more willing to compete for a big win than the men.

Competition, risk, and security go hand-in-hand, and this experiment was proof that being competitive and a risk-taker are learned traits. It also says some interesting (and unsettling) things about patriarchal societies and helps to prove that risk-taking can be learned to be a value for women in other cultures.

It is notable that the Profit Motive that seems to character-ize entrepreneurs most effectively is that they don't value security as much as someone who enjoys being an employee; they have a willingness to accept risk and forego assured profit for a chance to have greater long-run profits. This can be learned and can shift depending on time, place, and societal pressures. But given the extremes that the authors of *The Why Axis* had to go to find an exception to women's values of preferring security to taking a risk that could result either in failure or a big win, indicate it wouldn't be an easy process to change this characteristic in our society.

Personally, just like Ron knew that he was an entrepreneur early on, I knew that I was as well, although, I haven't been as successful in my endeavors as Ron. But at times in my life a guar-anteed paycheck has been more valuable to me than the risk. In fact, it wasn't until I gained the stability of my relationship with my wife as well as her encouragement that I gained the confidence that I needed to take the risks that I knew that I wanted to take.

Commuter Rituals

As a native Kansan transplanted to Washington, DC, one of the most interesting aspects of living on the East Coast was that com-muting to and from work has its own rituals, customs, and even tribes of sorts.

In Washington, DC, a few of the rituals are that people on the escalators stand to the right, and walkers pass on the left. (You'll frequently hear people shout, "Walk left, stand right!" during tourist season.) When on the Metro, the first one to sit on a bench seat is supposed to move all of the way over to the window, and there is no talking—none—and people next to the door must exit the train briefly at all stops to let others behind them exit easily to their destination; also eye contact should be kept to a minimum, and what few pregnant ladies there are get seats. And those are just some of the expectations for behavior when commuting on the Metro.

Slug lines in DC and the surrounding metro area—that stretch at least as far down as far as Richmond, VA—have their own subculture that can seem quite bizarre, but these rituals are also intriguing because of the interesting and almost spontaneous nature of the "market" that is full of profit motive for the riders and the drivers alike.

First, let's look at the interesting lives of the slugger. If you don't know what a "slug line" is, it's a type of formalized hitchhiking. The riders don't pay a fair, but in exchange for picking up the sluggers the driver gets to take advantage of the "High Occupancy Vehicle" lanes for their commute.

Before we get into the Profit Motive, which is interesting, of course, I want to talk about the rituals a bit, because while they might not be bizarre, per-se, they are interesting and, as we will see later, driven by Profit Motive.

In order to catch a slug line into work, the community has agreed on pick-up and drop-off points. A driver pulls into the parking lot where the sluggers are lined up. A "Caller" is out a few feet in front of the line and that is where the drivers pulls their car too. The driver tells the caller his destination—one of the agreed-upon stops—and how many people they can take. If the caller is going to that destination they yell to the line how many people are still needed and where they are going. Then the new passengers get in the car and drive off to the destination. If the caller had not going to that destination the driver yells out the place and the number of other riders he can take and that group of people get into the car and the caller stays in his or her position to wait for the next driver. Once in the car, the riders are expected not to talk. They are expected not to mention the temperature. They are expected not to mention the driving. They have a seat, and that is it. After the caller has left the line, the next person in line assumes the role and the process begins again.

I know people who have successfully slugged all the way into Washington, DC, from Richmond, VA, for years. That means that the demand is there for both the drivers and riders—and the drivers have saved each of the riders thousands of dollars each year. It is an amazing, unofficial system that spontaneously occurred because people have coinciding Profit Motives.

No money is exchanged, but there is an exchange of value. Sluggers pay with their time in line and loss of choice, and the driver pays for the car and gas, but they both gain time. The Profit Motive is gaining time, and what people pay with to gain that profit is their loss of choice, but it is a lower motivating factor than the "time" that is saved.

Win-win solutions are what free markets are all about, and this spontaneous commuting market of slug lines is a perfect example of how these win-wins are created.

But it doesn't necessarily take a market need for Profit Motive to show up. The rituals that have spontaneously occurred on Metro trains provide their own "profit" to make the commute more valuable for everyone—like a mutual treaty.

There are rules on Metro signs when entering the train station, on the platforms and even in the train cars about eating, drinking, and wearing headphones. While some people break the rules of course, usually they are followed, and even without the rules most people wouldn't need to have any rules stated to subscribe to this social contract. The reason is fairly simple: a desire for comfort. Being quiet doesn't save you any money, being quiet doesn't get anyone to their destination faster, but it does increase the comfort of those around you. That's the payment, and it's also the reward. It is interesting to watch, and it is at its most interesting when tourists or newbies from Kansas are introduced into the equation.

Newbies will often just observe first. They might only observe for a few a stops, or they might observe for a full week. However, at some point they will usually speak up and ask someone sitting next to them about the weird silence of a metro car full of commuters. The person that they speak too often quickly explains the rules of the commute, and then they resume their commute in silence.

Tourists are a different story. They usually act like they are in a zoo saying, "Hey! Why is everyone so quite in here. Is nobody in this town friendly?" The answer at the time is almost always a stone-cold wall of silence, or a snippy four-letter retort, which tends to reinforce the questioner's thoughts about his fellow riders, but it is just the fastest way to get the tourist to conform.

There is also another group of commuters using public transportation who like abusing the fact that there is a captive audience. Beggars, scammers, buskers, and preachers have all been known to use the commute as a time to take advantage of the quiet environment. (Note: they're probably more common in New York, which relies more on public transportation than DC.)

The takeaway here is that commuting is awful for everyone, but identifying the motivations that underlie the actions of commuters can make for good practice, like the new dynamically priced commuting lanes. If commuters are willing to pick up strangers and put them into their car in order to get someplace faster and more conveniently, it is also likely that others would pay for the privilege.

And these dynamically priced lanes are now starting to pop up around the country. Kind of like HOV lanes, dynamically priced lanes are usually separate from the normal lanes. The prices in these lanes vary with the level of congestion in the normal lanes. If the normal traffic is free flowing the cost for a segment of a few miles might be as low as $1, but as traffic starts increasing that same segment might increase to $4 or even more. This has proved to be very lucrative and helps both the normal flow of traffic and the new users of the dynamically priced lanes. Interestingly, I don't think that any of these new dynamically priced commuting lanes have been implemented by state or local governments, possibly because of perceived unfairness, but instead it has only been private companies that have figured out how to leverage this demand.

Employees, Coworkers, and Government Bureaucrats

A business is in business to make money, but depending on the incentives set up by the company, employees can actually work against the bottom line. They aren't intending to sabotage the company; they can just be maximizing their own profit motive.

Employees are people. I know that might not seem to be necessary to say, but economists are sometimes accused of looking past this fact and just looking that the numbers. It isn't just economists thinking this way, In large corporations individual employees can also be easy to forget. However, it is their incentives that can drive the bottom line of a company.

The basic Profit Motive of an employee is to make money, but unless a job is commission-based that might not mean that their incentive is to maximize the bottom line of the company. Having employees work for a "commission" isn't always the best way to build a long-term market for your company, and commissions introduce risk that employees, as we discussed earlier, might not want to bear.

Why would an employee be motivated to stay late for an additional sale or filing more paperwork if they aren't going to be fired and will make the same amount of money if they leave according to their normal schedule since there is no overtime pay? The answer is that many aren't. But some employees would stay late, in order to earn more respect from their colleagues and boss and hopefully a promotion at some point. In some jobs, though, the odds of getting a promotion or moving up in the organization is so low that this incentive doesn't exist.

The people senior to me at my first real job on Capitol Hill are still there ten years later. Fortunately, I identified that the odds of improving my place in the office were very low early on, but if I were still there today, my incentive to work hard, innovatively, or take on additional responsibilities would likely be very low.

There are ways to change this lack of motivation though. One is to always have the threat of being fired hanging over someone's head. (So that isn't a profit; it's just avoiding a loss.) It isn't a good approach, but it will work at least for a short time. However, in addition to the morale-killing aspect of that, the constant threat of firing people also increases the "risk" factor that risk-averse employees don't like.

The other, more productive (and right) way is to give ownership of the company to the employees. This motivation can be done in a startup by giving employees real buy in like giving away stock options or a buy in that is merely created from the culture. One of the keys to a successful startup is to create an aura of possible ownership and excitement. That excitement helps a startup hire smart people at below market wages. The atmosphere of anticipation is fun to be around and can help convince people to work a few extra hours. When entrepreneurs learn to hand the "idea" over to their employees, they give everyone the chance to participate in building the company.

Some of the best companies do this by giving a mix of "all of the above." In fact, to help insure the success of a business of any size, it is important to understand the wants and needs, the Profit Motive, of your employees as well as the people that you want to hire. Even more important to put into action, although it's very basic to understand, is that employees have their own motivation for profit that must be accounted for and harnessed. The importance of this understanding isn't just important for business owners or managers. It is also important when attempting to understand your coworkers. Despite the fact that you and your coworkers might appear the same to an accountant or a shareholder, the truth is that people in similar jobs at the same company are still different people. Again, this part isn't rocket science, but it is important to remember that people all vary. In the context of this book, these differences are important because individuals have different profit motives.

One person in a job might want to get home to be with their family, one person might want to leave early for a date, another might want to stay late for the overtime money, and someone else might want to work late to get the next promotion. If you understand the needs and wants of your coworkers you might be able to navigate the complex twists and turns of office politics better than someone else.

Let's do a quick thought experiment and attempt to navigate the politics of a five-person office, when all employees have different motivations while trying to secure a promotion.

Thought Experiment: Examining Different Motives

Steve, Landon, Anaya, Sarah, and Tom all work on team at Acme Inc. Steve wants a promotion, Landon needs more money, Anaya wants to get home to her family, Sarah wants more money, and Tom is in a new relationship and is going out every night.

If Steve wants a promotion, and understands that his teammates all have different motivations from his, he can more easily secure his promotion. First, to secure a promotion, he will need to impress the company (upper-level management). To do that Steve will want to increase the profit of the company increase their profit motive to keep him and promote him. Second, he should get his team behind him. This can be the tough part, because it is more likely out of Steve's hands. This is where navigating the dangerous political waters of an office more adeptly can come in handy. If Steve proposes, or volunteers for any new projects he needs to attempt to exclude the people who don't value having more work to do, or at least give them the chance to self-exclude. For instance, if Steve picks Anaya or Tom he could be in trouble because they might sabotage the project, either consciously or subconsciously.

If they can't be excluded, Steve might attempt to find another way for his not-so-willing-to-work teammates to fulfill their Profit Motive. Or, if he can't exclude them or convince them to self-exclude, then Steve might need to figure out another way to get a promotion altogether in order to avoid sabotage.

Office politics aren't usually fun for anyone, largely because of differing Profit Motives, but understanding them and attempting to work with them instead of against them can help make a bad situation better.

A bad situation that is not likely to get better is interacting with government employees. In fact, this is a reason I've spent most of my career attempting to limit the number of government employees there are. This shouldn't be taken as an accusation that bad people work for the government. That is untrue. It shouldn't be a taken as a statement that unqualified people work for the government. This is also untrue. The problem with government employees is that the motivations in their jobs are to either spend my tax money (or my kids' future tax money) on things without proper vetting, or they are motivated to restrict spending despite the situation.

If government employees didn't have personal Profit Motives, most programs would work amazingly better. But people are motivated, and these motivations change the way that they perform their duties. For instance, the employees that work for Medicaid aren't incentivized under the current system to make sure that they are reaching the people that the system was originally designed to take care of, the people at or below the poverty level. They are just tasked with signing up as many people as possible.

I'm not taking a position here on whether the expansion is good or not—or whether or not the staff at the Medicaid office are competent or not. But if the Medicaid program is effective and successful, and the people that run it are competent and effective, then most people would agree that the people who need the program and services the most are the ones at the bottom of the economic ladder. However, since the program has been available to that population for a number of years, the process of signing eligible people up and the easy part of educating the public about Medicaid eligibility has already been implemented. In fact, according to New England Journal of Medicine paper, across the country an average of 40 percent of the Medicaid-eligible population still hadn't signed up before the expansion.

> Three key results emerge from this analysis. First, partic-
> ipation rates are far from ideal, with a national average of
> 61.7% of eligible individuals. Second, Medicaid participa-
> tion is highly variable, with rates ranging from just under
> 44% in Oklahoma, Oregon, and Florida to 80% in Massa-
> chusetts and 88% in the District of Columbia. Third, the
> states that will have the greatest number of newly eligible
> adults under health care reform have, if anything, been
> historically worse (but not significantly so) at finding and
> keeping eligible adults enrolled in Medicaid (regression
> coefficient, -0.46; 95% confidence interval, -1.13 to 0.21).[33]

That means that to reach the parts of the community, which is a population of people that is also always in flux and who haven't enrolled yet, is going to be hard. However, both for the politicians bureaucrats running the program the incentive is not for them to ask for more money to sign up this hard to reach population of people, because the Return-on-Investment is going to be lower than what they are used to (gorilla style door-by-door outreach is slow and expensive).

Therefore, when the Affordable Care Act expanded Medicaid, it made complete sense that the growth rate of the program dramatically increased. The Medicaid office now had a completely new population of people to target, but tragically the addition of a new, "richer," population of eligible individuals means that even less attention was paid to attempting to enroll the 40 percent of eligible people that were truly in need before the expansion. So, even if you support the expansion, if you follow the incentives of the politicians and bureaucrats in charge of running the programs then the expansion of Medicaid came at the expense of forgetting about the neediest and instead provided a new incentive for these individuals to focus on the newly eligible population—the low hanging fruit.

Bureaucrats aren't judged based on their bottom line or how skillful they are. They are often judged on how much work they do, not the effectiveness or value of that work. It is kind of like judging a business based on how many products are added to their inventory in a given year instead of how many new products they sold. It doesn't really mean anything to add products if people don't want them. Similarly, just adding people to a program doesn't mean that a program is more or less effective. It just means that more people are in the program and that more money is being spent. The poorest are still likely deserving of the help they need, but instead of insuring the poorest get the help they need the focus becomes merely adding people to the roles. For instance, in the only scientific study done regarding Medicaid, the results showed that merely being enrolled in Medicaid created no difference in health outcomes in the first two years. In fact, according to the paper there was, "no significant effect of Medicaid coverage on the prevalence or diagnosis of hypertension or high cholesterol levels or on the use of medication for these conditions.[34] Therefore, it would seem that if a major program like Medicaid would be reformed, then that reform would focus on making the program more effective right?

Nope. The political profit of spending more money per-person isn't as high as spending more money on more people. So the end result is that when Medicaid when through its last major reform, as part of the Affordable Care Act, instead of fixing the effectiveness of the program the focus was primarily on expanding the ineffective program.

And, as predicted, enrollment has grown. The Kaiser Family Foundation tracks growth rates of Medicaid enrollees and they noted that the growth rates of Medicaid varied dramatically in states that expanded vs. states that didn't after the passage of ObamaCare. In states that expanded the program it grew at a rate of 12.9 percent, and it grew at only 2.6 percent in states that did not participate in Medicaid expansion. What is the value of expanding a program almost 5 times faster if nobody's health improves? Of course that wasn't a question that the reformers asked themselves.

This doesn't happen only in controversial areas of government spending like Medicaid. A few years ago the Parks Service published a phone app that cost them a ton of money. Before a business creates an app they would normally think about how the application would help increase their profit, but the government doesn't have those same incentives. The employees making these decisions don't have the same incentives, so they aren't forced to prove any potential benefit. When money is free, the answer, or Profit Motive, of everyone in the decision chain is more.

Reversing this Profit Motive of many government bureaucrats is nearly impossible, but as voters we can focus on the elected officials who let this happen under their watch. The real answer is to limit government to the smallest unit that is necessary. We can debate how small that government should be, but it is unlikely that "bigger" is the right answer.

How Others Attempt to Leverage Your Profit Motive

I have already made the point that capitalism is a win-win, but it is the job of the marketing department to convince you, or any potential buyer, that the value of a good is high enough to create that win-win solution.

To put it another way, we are consistently forced to make decisions about value, but those decisions are rarely being made in a vacuum, which gives salesman and marketers opportunities to increase your perceived value of their product. The infomercial for the Snuggy, the blanket with sleeves, is a perfect example of this. The actors in the commercial wrestle show how they with their ordinary blankets over and over. Before that commercial how many people thought to themselves, "Hey, my blanket is a pain!"? Probably not that many, but the Snuggy models were able to convince enough people that it was such a big problem that it became a hit product with good sales that continue today, years after the product's initial introduction.

All infomercials operate on this premise, but even the normal 30-second variety of commercials do as well. Most beer commercials try to convey the idea that people who buy their beer are cool, suave, or hip. Investment commercials try to convey that they are the caring or intelligent solution to saving money. Drug commercials try to show that the drugs can be widely used for all kinds of people. Commercials are there to build up the value of their product and their demand.

It isn't just on TV though. The hairdresser who sells you hairspray or shampoo is leveraging an opportunity to convince their clients that they can get more value out of a certain hair product. A waiter might try to convince people that a "special" provides a better value than other meals on a menu. Or a gadget retailer might attempt to sell gadget insurance that allows you to protect your investment. The secret is to identify when someone is attempting to leverage your personal Profit Motives, effectively de-leveraging their position.

I mentioned the gadget insurance because it is one that affects me personally. As an economist, I always advise people against these plans, and in fact they are treated by the stores that sell them as almost a pure profit source. First, before you make a claim for something like a new phone, you have to pay a deductible. Second, you probably won't get a new phone. Third, your phone claim has to be covered. But those aren't the most important reasons to the store. Those are the positive aspects of the product to the insurance underwriting company, but the most valuable part of the insurance for stores is that it is something that they can sell that they don't need to hold in inventory since everything else that they have in stock actually costs them money the longer that it sits in the store. The fact that these plans are a huge profit center for the businesses that sell them is why they push them at almost every stage of the sale, but they are also leveraging a time that the buyer is likely making a larger purchase, and the buyer will likely want to protect their investment and profit (increased quality of life) from the new gadget.

If it isn't a good investment, and the store is leveraging a time that I might want to protect myself and profit that I just gained from buying my technology, then why did I purchase insurance on my last phone?

I understood what was going on. I understood that my routine phone use is very, very, very, hard on phones. So after several years of experience I wasn't purchasing insurance; I was purchasing a future replacement phone when I eventually broke mine. In addition to that, I bought one of the more expensive phones, so the potential savings was even larger for me.

It turns out that my decision was correct. I dropped my phone in a parking a lot less than the year before my insurance expired; when I broke the screen, my phone was replaced almost the next day. I might not have saved as much as the advertising said that I could save, and I didn't receive a new phone, but if I had purchased my phone from Craigslist, eBay, or another second-hand market, I would have paid more money and had results that weren't as assured. The insurance company was attempting to leverage my Profit Motive, but because of my experience and knowledge of my own history I had leveraged theirs by buying the insurance.

Paying attention to your own Profit Motives can have other benefits too. In recent years, several websites have popped up that allow you to bet on weight loss and other things that require impulse control. The point of these websites is that if you want to leverage your own Profit Motive, you should put money at stake—or gamify the situation. This can done with things like quitting smoking as well as saving more money.

The problem with accomplishing at least these three goals—smoking, saving money, and losing weight—is that the "profit" from accomplishing them isn't immediate. If you quit smoking, you probably won't immediately notice the years that you add to your life. If you lose weight this month, the immediate effect is really just more expense from the need to buy new clothes. The health benefits won't manifest themselves for years. And, it is basically the same thing with saving money. It's hard to convince people of the benefits of saving money early in life when the alternative is having cooler stuff now. That's why if we give ourselves some way to profit now, leveraging our Profit Motive, we then accomplish our goals with more ease.

Bringing It Together: The Collective

When you add up the individual Profit Motives of everyone, you get the world that we interact with. The motives of the business owners, the employees, the coworkers, and the government bureaucrats all change and affect almost everything that we do, see, and buy. The motivations of individuals are roundly under-appreciated.

For instance, communism is a whole political system based on ignoring the Profit Motive of individuals. The only way that communism is even close to viable is if a Profit Motive doesn't exist. But it does and is what breaks communism when countries have attempted to implement it. Profit Motive means that if an employee can't earn more money they are likely to seek profit else-where. That means that they might figure out how to work the least amount as possible and put the least amount of effort into their job. In other words, increase their profit in the only ways available to them. Plenty of sad managers understand that asking people to do more without the promise of more is a failing strategy.

The actions of large corporations owe something to the mis-sion of the organization, but the overall output of a company really just boils down to the individual actions of all of the employees. How is the salesperson motivated to sale more day after day, week after week, and year after year? Do they get a bonus? Are they competing with their peers? Are they driven to move up the lad-der or get a bigger region? Does the help desk earn more for good ratings? Does that mean that the nicer but less technically able person will get better outcomes, and what does that mean for the competence of the help desk?

Profit Motive also causes one of the more annoying aspects of daily life, at least in mine, and likely yours: the drive people have to talk on conference calls and in meetings. Individuals often feel the need to express the fact that they are there at the meeting and helping drive the group forward. Their profit is that everyone knows that they are participating and, if they are smart, the hope to convince the companies leaders that they are helping to bring in their profit.

It is hard to have the Profit Motive of everyone in a company pointed toward the mission of a business all of the time, but when you are on the lookout for perverse incentives in a company, they then can be found. One of the biggest ways to leverage Profit Motive is just to understand what each individual in a company wants.

Like the example that we used above in the thought experiment, not everyone requires more money to move closer to their goals. Giving someone who wants more time with their family a more flexible schedule might be more important to them. Profit Motive also doesn't need to be micro-managed, although managed correctly, an efficient business might be able to let their employees pick their own most valuable way forward—perhaps a cafeteria-style benefit plan or a Management By Objective (MBO) performance evaluation. More money vs. flexibility. More responsibility vs. flexibility. The options might be as endless as individuals are individual, but it is a simple way to quickly provide employees more than they might have gotten from a simple monetary raise.

That type of realization and reaction is still just the start. Individual Profit Motives are literally everywhere, and when you start seeing them, more and more of the actions of the people around you start making sense.

PROFIT MAN

Like any individual, Profit Man has individual goals. That doesn't mean that Profit Man is greedy, but it means that if he isn't being greedy, he is angling for something else.

Maybe that something else is just a better relationship with his mother-in-law, or, more likely, it is a to give himself a greater opportunity to make money down the road. Nobody wants to do business with the guy that stepped all over them just to get to a client. Profit Man has an eye out for the future, and that means that he is often very cordial and quick to please people.

As an employee, Profit Man is great, as a friend he is loyal, as a business partner there is nobody better. His motivations, his individual motivations, are focused on his long-run goal, and that is making money. Burning bridges, losing allies, and making enemies of people don't help him reach his long-run goal.

Not surprisingly, Profit Man also doesn't like gambling. He isn't a fan of risk, but he is willing to accept risk when it is necessary and everything that can be known about a situation is known. Profit Man is one of the easiest people to deal with because his actions are almost always predictable.

8

Family

HAVE YOU EVER ASKED YOURSELF WHY a love interest or spouse is with you? That question is asking about their Profit Motive. In other words, just like we should ask in every situation, you are asking what your partner is getting out of the relationship? What is their profit?

Thankfully, at least for me, the "profit" in a relationship isn't usually money or wealth. Profit in a relationship is often something less tangible. For instance, I wanted a teammate. I wanted someone who could support my drive to forge a path that was not likely to be as traditional as many Americans. I wanted a partner who would work with me so that we could accomplish our dreams. I found that in my wife, Andrea.

What did Andrea want? Again, thankfully it wasn't money. I wasn't on a path to make a lot of money. It also wasn't looks—I am not exactly Elmer Fudd, but George Clooney probably wouldn't be the actor that would play me in a movie either.

Andrea wanted somebody with drive and the entrepreneurial spark. I had that, although it also manifests itself often as bad dad jokes, random wires around the house, and of course dumb purchases that are hard to explain. Andrea wanted to be a part of the excitement, and together we have built a great business, family, and relationship together.

While we both gain from these long-term "profit" centers, there are also other pieces that drive relationships. I want a teammate, but in order to keep my teammate I need to talk to her. I need to make sure that she is okay and that she is taken care of. Fortunately, I also want to do things for her, which helps, but if I want to maintain my team and therefore my profit. I need to make sure that my partner is doing alright.

From her side of it, if she wants to continue to see the entrepreneurial spark she has to be there when there are failures. She need to look out for wires every once in a while. And, within reason, she needs to understand that a few dumb investments might be a part of the process.

This give and get style of relationship can be very profitable for both sides.

There is also a way to use this innate Profit Motive within relationships as well. Most people understand that if you want something from your partner, such as wanting to watch an action movie rather than a chick flick, or take a beach vacation instead of museum-filled tourist vacation, or just to have sex, then you better be on your partner's good side.

Dr. Bob Emmons, a friend of mine, calls this last one a "Sex Bank." Bob is a board-certified psychiatrist with a solo private practice in Burlington. He is part-time clinical associate professor of psychiatry at the University of Vermont where he teaches in the areas of psychoanalytic psychotherapy and ethics.

Bob and I were talking about motives and relationships when he started discussing his idea that there is a "Sex Bank" that men should think about (this works the other way too, but it was two men talking together). If you want sex, but there is no money in your sex bank, then you might be out of luck. To take the thought experiment further your spouse might even give you credit, but eventually that credit is going to run out. But, if instead you do things to help out (like I might help my wife with one of her chores in addition to doing mine to save her some time), I might be banking "profit" in my sex bank. Brilliant.

This is more than just picking up after yourself though. For example, as Bob also pointed out to me, if your wife wants to go to a romantic comedy and you object, and she complains, and you finally give in, you haven't actually banked anything in your sex bank. You have rejected her idea and only grudgingly given in. On the other hand, if you could (and you should) make your mind up at the beginning, you then might be able to bank something in your sex bank.

I like the idea of a "Sex Bank," but the idea is bigger. Realistically everyone, every company, and every organization has one bank or several of some sort, and they want deposits into that bank. This "Bank" idea is also discussed by Stephen Covey in his book, *The Seven Habits of Highly Effective People*. In his book Stephen Covey discusses the idea of an Emotional Bank.[35] Covey's Emotional bank and Dr. Emmon's Sex Bank are really just both banks—which are ways of saving up our profit.

Most of the time this type of relationship where banking occurs or a "give and get" is ok. But just to be clear, things can go off of the rails if the "profit" is something harmful, like drinking, when the relationship can be harmed as both sides seek to enable, or provide, profit for each other. It is very easy to imagine a conversation that goes something like this,

Person A: "I want to go drinking."

Person B: "No, not tonight."

Person A: "Come on."

Person B: *Thinking about possibly banking something*, "Okay."

Now the drinking continues, and "Person A" might feel like they owe something to Person B and maybe that thing will be more drinking. This can become a bad spiral.

Moderate drinking is all right most of the time, but if two people in a relationship are feeding off of each in a way that causes them to drink more than they might ordinarily, that could be a recipe for a broken relationship at best and even a tragic end at worst.

It isn't just our relationships with our significant others that are affected by Profit Motives in our families. Our relationships with our kids, our parents, and the family unit as a whole are all affected.

Kids are almost all about Profit Motives. They throw something on the floor, you pick it up. They throw it on the floor, you pick it up. They throw it back onto the floor, and now they have your attention, and they have a game. The next time that they want attention, they are likely to throw things on the floor.

B.F. Skinner had a lot to say about behavior and reinforcement of that behavior, but one conclusion that he often returned to is that people respond better to positive reinforcement than to negative reinforcement. Profit. In *Walden Two*, Skinner writes, "We are only just beginning to understand the power of love because we are just beginning to understand the weakness of force and aggression."

We, my wife and I, have found that this is true with our kids. Punishment can help stop a situation at the time, but it doesn't do anything for us in the long run. To guide our kids, we look toward rewarding them. Skinner has a reason for this too: "A person who has been punished is not less inclined to behave in a given way; at best, he learns how to avoid punishment."

Of course the simple way to think about it is just that kids are profit-seeking, too. They want love, they want attention, they want candy, chocolate, and toys. In our family we don't punish our kids for not eating their dinner; instead we reward them with desert if they do eat their food. This has turned out to be powerful. One of my daughters will actually—without too much protest—eat things that make her gag (like chicken) just to get a little desert. Putting that goal out there for her is all that she needs to motivate her. Interestingly, even at their early ages they have already seemed to pick up on the basic lessons, and they attempt to use rewards to motivate us, like bartering good behavior or chores for things that they want.

Rewards need to be done correctly though. A lot of families use rewards to help teach their kids. The research that provides a lot of the background to how and why we would do this is from B.F. Skinner and his book *Science and Human Behavior*:

> Operant conditioning shapes behavior as a sculptor shapes a lump of clay. Although at some point the sculptor seems to have produced an entirely novel object, we can always follow the process back to the original undifferentiated lump, and we can make the successive stages by which we return to this condition as small as we wish. At no point does anything emerge which is very different from what preceded it. The final product seems to have a special unity or integrity of design, but we cannot find a point at which this suddenly appears. In the same sense, an operant is not something which appears full grown in the behavior of the organism. It is the result of a continuous shaping process.[36]

So, in my family "operant conditioning" comes in two forms. First, when a certain habit or action is being conditioned (like potty training) rewards come right at the time of the desired action. After the action and reward relationship has been established, we then change the schedule of reward (or large reward) by moving to a chart system. Kids, and in Skinner's research, pigeons, pick up on these rewards very quickly.

If done wrong, or your kid is too smart, things can a little awry. B.F. Skinner used to be able to teach his pigeons to walk in figure 8s in minutes, but teaching each of daughters was more of a lesson in patience than anything else. And, a lot of it comes down to rewarding the right actions at the right times. Do you reward an accident if it happened while trying to do the right thing? What if you aren't in a position to offer an immediate reward? How much time do you spend teaching the baby sitter the benefits of a variable and immediate reward schedule?

The answer of course is that you just do the best that you can in the circumstances you are in. But one way to remember to focus is, for instance, to remember to remind your spouse of the greater amount of money that you will save on diapers the faster you are through potty training. Give yourself a Profit Motive.

One economist friend of mine was having trouble potty training* their daughter. The wife threw up her hands in defeat and handed the job to the father, the economist. He stepped in and had his daughter performing almost right away. He was giving her candy when she went to the potty, and it was working, and working quickly. However, one time when she went to the potty and earned her candy, she went back into the bathroom again to go a bit more and came back out for more candy. She was gaming the system for more candy-profit.

The correct reward schedule is important, but if you want to read more about operant conditioning I would refer you Skinner's work. For us, the important thing is that Skinner proves that even pigeons will change action if they profit from that change.

There is more to parenting a child with Profit Motive in mind. We, okay maybe this one is primarily on me, also attempt to instill a higher Profit Motive in our daughters and we find that this also helps them deal with others.

Yaron Brook, the President of the Ayn Rand Center, gave a speech one time about the lessons that we teach our kids, that I found very interesting and helpful. This is a paraphrase of what Yaron said:

When your kid, little Bobby, is playing on the playground the social norm or social pressure is to teach them to "share." But if one of little Bobby's friends parent came up and asked you to borrow your keys you probably wouldn't just quickly hand over your possession to them. The better thing to do is to teach little Bobby to trade. Then when one of his friends comes up to him on the playground they might be able to work out a mutual beneficial deal.

---

* I realized I'm repeatedly referring to "the potty" in an academic discussion of incentives; deal with it.

I have attempted to explain this to a few other parents, and they just give me the eye like I am being callous and that "sharing" should be the norm. However, in my house trading has become an amazing solution. Before we started the "trading" approach my eldest would take toys from the youngest and just run away. We would always track her down and discuss sharing, but the damage to the youngest was already done, and the wailing and tears were already there. Now, when she takes something we remind her that she needs to trade. And, we enforce the mutually beneficial part of trading which means that if the person being traded with doesn't like the trade, the trade doesn't happen.

It is fun to watch this process work out and sometimes even break down, but now that trading is in place we get to avoid many of the fights that forced altruism brings up, and our daughters have learned about profit.

Besides sharing, another age-old right-of-passage is the lemonade stand. Running a lemonade stand is many kid's introduction to business—at least in the US. For those readers that never ran, worked at, or set up a lemonade stand, it goes something like this:

1. Set up a table

2. Set lemonade on the table

3. Make signs to promote the lemonade

4. Profit

The main goal of having the lemonade stand is to transact something for money and therefore learn entrepreneurship. The cost of the lemonade may not even be under the cost of actual production. The labor isn't really a thought when the pricing is created. The point is to learn all of these things and the potential profit helps drive the lessons.

The lemonade stand is an amazing teacher. It teaches preparation, marketing, timing, cleanliness, staff, hard work, and a bit of finance. It also teaches investment and the time preference of money (profit). To start a lemonade stand takes money. We had our girls pay for it, and of course they wanted other things besides what was needed for the stand, but as we nudged them toward the right business decisions they slowly came around. Seeing that a dollar invested now might be worth two dollars tomorrow is one of the primary differentiators of being an entrepreneur—the ability to delay profit.

In recent years a new phenomenon has appeared: the nonprofit lemonade stand that is making the lessons from the lemonade stand harder for many to teach. In fact, when my neighbor and I recently helped our kids with their lemonade stand, we were confronted by someone asking about what charity we were raising funding for.

> *Lemonade Client*: "What charity are your girls raising money for?"
>
> *Neighbor*: "Um, I am sorry. I didn't hear your question."
>
> *Lemonade Client*: "What charity will the proceeds go to?"
>
> *Neighbor:* "Ummmmmm."
>
> *Me:* "The girls are keeping the money. We are teaching them entrepreneurship. Our break-even point is 50 sales. Can I interest you in a lemonade?"
>
> She bought a lemonade, but had a bit of snarl as she walked away.

Nonprofit lemonade stands begin like other stands, but instead of keeping the money at the end of the day the kids give the money to a charity. A charitable lemonade transaction misses the point of the lemonade stand, which is ordinarily sales and entrepreneurship. Instead it teaches charity. That isn't necessarily a bad lesson, but the whole point of the exercise is to teach entrepreneurship.

The problem isn't necessarily the charity, but they change the Profit Motive that lowers the drive to run the stand. Earning money at a lemonade stand involves taking in quarters and giving people lemonade. Every time that one of the kids running the lemonade takes a quarter from someone they can actually feel the profit coming in. However, if the kids are raising money for something or someone else, every time they handle the quarter they know that it isn't theirs. The Profit Motive dissipates and the value of the whole exercise is diminished—like the potty chart described earlier.

While I wouldn't suggest treating kids like science experiments, I would encourage everyone to treat their kids like adults and pay attention early on to their motivations. Positive reinforcement, such as profit, is a strong driver that can help further motivate kids. You can also easily teach the wrong lessons if you forget to think about the signals that you are sending.

Working with your kids and attempting to provide the motivations is fairly easy, but family dynamics can get complicated when everyone has to start interacting. The desire to profit is still there, but when dealing with family "ego," as a form of profit, can become a problem. For instance, as a younger generation in a family ages causing the relationships to change, it is hard to treat a peer as anything less than a peer, an older family member can easily have their ego hurt when treated as an equal. This is a case of "profit" and "ego" colliding.

Ego growth can be a form of profit, but it in general it is a dangerous form of profit since an over-inflated ego can easily become self-defeating, And, this issue can be worse in families. In families, there is a pecking order—and that order is primarily defined by age. So, if a younger family member is trying to talk to an older family member as a peer, but they both have "ego" as a part of their profit mix then one of them could get hurt by almost any perceived slight which is very likely in a multi-generational family get-together.

Here is another example from my own family, mainly because it was a blatant case of not reading the situation correctly. Like many families there is an argumentative side to my family that often leads us to think that we are right, and that anyone who thinks that we are wrong must be wrong and irrational. This thought process led to an argument with my grandmother in which the fallout was that we stopped talking for more than six months.

Why? Because the profit gain (enhancement to the ego) was valued too highly for both sides.

It all started because of an argument that we were having about illegal aliens. I had called grandma up on the way home late from work. Before stopping by home, I pulled into a 7-Eleven parking lot while talking to her, and I decided to stay in the car to finish the debate (argument) before going inside to pick up some beer after the long day. While the conversation started off as cordial, it quickly turned into a back and forth and a battle of wits. We don't need to re-litigate the facts of the debate (I was right, of course), but the end result was that each of us was seeking the "profit" of a win. We were thinking that we could win the other's respect. Since we were both seeking the same profit, and holding out for that profit, the conversation ended in a hung up phone.

In the heat of the moment the fight and ending made sense. In retrospect the better "profit" might have been to give in and help maintain the relationship.

After the call ended, our Profit Motive of wanting to gain or maintain pride in ourselves didn't end. What finally ended the silence was an inflection point and a time that seemed like there was less pride to be lost by reaching out. It worked and we began talking again. I called her because we were expecting our first child.

While I am not even really a fan of writing in the first person this story is important to tell, because when gaining "pride" or enhancing our "ego" are the Profit Motive, the fight can quickly get out of control. When money is involved it is easy to run through a profit analysis, but our ego or pride are limitless in size. Naturally some people have very little ego or pride, but if that ego or pride were to start growing. there is no limit to how large an ego can grow, and there is no limit to how pride you can feel. Therefore, gaining pride or building our ego means less. If there is no upward limit then each "unit" (not really a thing) is worth less profit. This could—and should—mean that losing ego means less too, but that isn't often the case.

In part because of this weird effect, many people suggest that one of the worst things to do is a family business or even doing any business with family.

I learned this when I was fairly young. I wrecked my car, and my uncle fixed it. He paid for everything, and he did it quickly using his employees' time and his money to buy the parts. He then gave me a bill that was almost more than the car was worth. The problem from my end was that he had been helpful, so saying no was tough. The problem on his end was that the family knew that he had the resources and would have looked callous if he hadn't helped me. At the time I would have thought so too. (I wouldn't now.)

When I looked at the bill because I wondered how it had skyrocketed so high, I also knew that I needed to pay him back because I saw he had only charged me what he had paid to have it fixed, and now the family pressure was on me. It was a wild conundrum: The cost of the fix seemed too high, but the money had already been spent.

I slowly paid the debt for years, and my uncle eventually forgave a large portion of the remaining debt. But I am sure that at points he had some choice words for me, and I know that I had choice words for him. I know now that I was definitely in the wrong. He had helped me and spent money from his own pocket (which is also his family's pocket) to help me. In reality the problem wasn't really his fault or mine (okay, my slow payment was my fault). The real problem was that the family value on helping me was too high. He was going to help me at almost any cost, and then I was bound by the same rules to pay back for that help.

Don't do business with family. The incentives are horrible. Some people make it work, but given the many paths that life can take it is usually only a matter of time before someone's Profit Motive doesn't align with someone else's Profit Motive and that can cause trouble quickly.

Bringing a Family Together

As we have discussed, Profit Motives drive relationships with spouses, kids, and even extended family. If a spouse is failing to get something out of a relationship that they want, that need should quickly be addressed. If not, their "bank" is going to quickly run out. It is also good to remember that we often over-value "ego," or our pride in our self or our self-esteem, which is of almost no use inside of the family unit, and really almost of no use out of it, but is something that many people put a high value on.

Also, kids are almost completely profit driven, and fortunately they often put a high value on things that have little financial value, such as small pieces of chocolate, shiny pennies, and stickers. This placement of high value on low-cost objects can really help parenting be taken to the next level.

The key for myself and familial Profit Motive is just being aware about how my actions are affecting the current and future Profit Motives of those around me. I want to teach my kids that their future desire to gain profit shouldn't just be about money, but also about love, education, and maybe even charity. Again, because money isn't usually involved, this can be harder to identify inside of a family unit.

In general, familial Profit Motives don't differ much from corporate or political motivations, but they do hit closer to home, and since they often don't involve money they can be harder to track. Whether you get scientific and discuss operative conditioning and reward schedules, or it's just a small tiff with another parent about a lemonade stand, recognizing that even inside of a family that Profit Motives exist is important.

PROFIT MAN

He can't always live in a board room, so sometimes Profit Man heads home to his family. Does he charge his family for every dinner that they consume? Does he charge them for hugs? Does he divvy up the electric bill or put a coin lock on the bathroom? No.

Profit Man knows that he is not likely to benefit financially from his family, but he can still be a family man. And Profit Man can profit emotionally from being with his family or recharge his batteries to earn more profit the next day. However, just because he isn't making money, doesn't mean that he isn't still thinking about profit. Profit Man is keeping track of favors, he is keeping track of conversations, chores, and just about everything. Fortunately, Profit Man likes to have a full bank, so he isn't calling in his bank chits very often.

Unlike the way he is at work, Profit Man isn't trying to get ahead. Unlike the way he is in his business, Profit Man isn't trying to make a sale. In general, while at home Profit Man is reaping the benefits of his hard work and sharing those benefits with his family.

9

To the Last Penny!

HIGHLY SUSPICIOUS OF MY WRITING A BOOK about how, to borrow a phrase, "Greed is good," a friend asked me: "What is the most radical critique of profit?" And his question was the last question that solidified my idea that Profit Motive is the primary driver of the world we live in.

The most radical critique that I could come up with would be if someone called making a profit immoral. Therefore, under this critique, profit would be considered bad, evil, anti-society, etc. To take it a step further, in a world that considered profit immoral, every product would necessarily be sold at cost. But what is "cost" of the labor? What is the cost of the management? What is the cost of the risk? As soon as people enter into the question of "cost," even the radical critique starts to fall apart and give way to the idea of Profit Motive.

When we look at even the most radical critique of profit, the problem that still exists at the end of the day is that someone needs to decide what someone else is worth and they need to decide how to value that person's time. It doesn't actually matter "who" asks those questions. But if that person doesn't consider the Profit Motive of the people that they are deciding the questions about, the answer will be wrong and the market would break.

Let's think about building a house in this anti-profit society. In order to build a house a builder needs wood, nails, a lot of other supplies, and labor. For now, let's assume that someone has figured out the "cost" for land and supplies. We are then left with identifying the value of labor. If the rule puts too low a value on workers' time, the employees might not show up to work because their motivation to work will be too low—or be trumped by other motivations. If the valuation of the laborer's time is too high, the price of the house will necessarily increase and demand will slump as buyers' motivations no longer provide support for that level of valuation.

And, even after these weighty decisions are made, the land developer's risk, value, or costs haven't been considered. How would the risk that a developer takes be valued? If that value is low, then development would slow down. If the value is high, then the market takes a different shape, perhaps causing a real estate bubble.

To look at these same decisions from even one more angle, consider that even if the government is making these decisions, the need to account for Profit Motive doesn't disappear. And the profit motive of the individual bureaucrat, the politician, and even the voter now must be accounted for as well. People are driven, people are motivated, and no amount of law will change that.

So, even if you consider financial profit as evil, people are still motivated by a Profit Motive of wanting a family or love, time, money, stability, vacations, sleep, health, community, and so forth. People need to be motivated to work, and those motivations vary for everyone.

The Stumbling Blocks

Entrepreneurs, businesses, families, and individuals need to focus on real long-run profits. Real long-run profits, personal and financial, are what make capitalism work and provide us the ability to look out for a Profit Motive instead of searching for a moral code. Looking for Profit Motive can help us understand the way a business runs or forecast the decisions a person is likely to make.

But, while it is evident that people are driven by profit, forecasting the actions of others because of this drive doesn't come without a few hiccups.

This "error" factor can lead to errors in forecasting a Profit Motive. One example of this error is in analyzing the behavior of Bernie Madoff. Bernie was caught running one of the biggest Ponzi schemes in the history of Ponzi schemes. He was taking money from rich investors, promising above-market returns, and paying them off with money from the newest investors. Some might point to the greed of Bernie Madoff and assume that he was merely an unchained Profit Man. However, as Bernie can now attest, this isn't true. Unless Profit Man values going to jail over money, family, or freedom, going to prison for life isn't something that Profit Man would seek.

Therefore, Bernie Madoff wasn't acting as Profit Man; he was just being greedy. That greed landed him in jail with a 150-year sentence. Bernie is a prime example of how profit motivation can be confused with other actions, but not all, or most, of the examples are so extreme. In fact, most examples are much more subtle and don't involve greed or illegal activities as much as a failure to fully understand all of the variables.

In fact, a good example of this is just to look at a business's accounting. Well, it might not be that easy, but there is an accounting rule-of-thumb saying that goes, "Profit is prince. Cash is king." The idea is that "profit" can be deceiving. If you turn a blind eye to what went into what your business is doing with its cash—or what goes into making that profit.

One of my good friends, (okay, he was best man at my wedding), Nicholas Buchanan cofounded a company a few years ago with the idea of helping businesses identify when they are making the right decisions. The company, BUCS Analytics, provides to their clients Big Data analytics software to use for service (SaaS) solutions. The one driving motivation for its use is—more profit—although they call their goal "value and performance."

They have basically created a software-based, decision-maker for their clients, or what I call a "Profit Man," to consult. This allows their clients to identify cash traps, identify how their client might be losing money on inventory, what products they should focus on, and even the marginal value of an employee. By giving their clients access to this virtual consultant they unlock the market for them. If they listen to his version of Profit Man, the only thing that would hold back a business at that point is the size of the market.

One of the generic problems Nick first helps clients solve is to calculate whether they're carrying too much inventory. For instance, if a company sells widgets, they need to a stock of widgets, but *when* do they need that stock, and how many do they need? Many companies will have too many widgets in stock at any given time, which means that they are losing money because the cash invested in the inventory could be invested in the market earning money as an investment, or it could be reinvested in a different part of the company (such as sales if Nick's software says the company is earning enough money from their salespeople). Too much inventory is an innocent mistake. You can do it defensively, or you might have too much inventory because of laziness, or as a result of nobody paying attention since it doesn't show up as waste on balance sheet. For people who aren't Profit Man, errors happen.

However, inventory is the low-hanging fruit. When trying to dig down and really look at "profit" you have to go further. So, at BUCs they are paying attention to things on a question-by-question basis, in real time. Their Profit Man knows when an answer is going to cost more than it will likely bring in—or isn't the most efficient use of a company's cash.

People don't realize what they are investing in to generate profit and that looking at profit without a constraint or investment is deceiving. It is the question of a lot of people that have inherited wealth. How rich are they, and did they generate wealth or did he inherit it all? Did they take the inheritance and earn an adequate return or did they start out rich and get a worse return than just putting the money in the market?

Take for an example a current client of mine that does work with Wal-Mart Stores, Inc. This is an actual example. Wal-Mart provides them $1.5 million of revenue a year. On that revenue they make 30 percent gross margin. After taking a further look at total cost they realize they lose another 10 percent of profit in returns and hidden costs. Still at 20 percent profit that is still pretty good, right? If that profit takes a quarter-million of investment, is that still good? I think most companies should get a 2 to 1 payback on working capital.

Now Wal-Mart has come back to them and said we can help grow your business with us 50 percent in the next year. To do so we need 120 day terms (in reality this become 130+ days). This is big numbers for my client. That is $750k of additional revenue. That is $150k of additional profit. What we help to identify is that is going to be $700k of additional investment making the total investment nearly $1 million. Is that still good profit? That client can reinvest that money into smaller clients and could possibly generate $2 million or they could diversify and disperse it to shareholders, etc.

Profit it is very important. But it needs to be looked at in relative terms to risk and return. Return on capital employed is the financial factor most correlated to value of a business. Those concepts need to be evaluated at the same level decisions are being made to make sure day to day decisions regarding profit are aligned with the goal of the business to generate value.

—Nicholas Buchannon, BucsAnalytics

From an interview I held with him on September 28, 2016

Profit Man is perfectly able to make decisions regarding profit. Profit Man is fully able to understand the future and the implications that his decisions will have both now and then. But regular people aren't Profit Men. We get distracted, we get greedy, we deal with imperfect knowledge or information, and that means that we make decisions that aren't always perfectly aligned with profit. As many have said, the most irrational assumption is that markets behave rationally.

The speed bumps in misguided Profit Motives don't just show up on a company's balance sheet though. If someone values time with family more than increased pay and thinks that a better job might be the path to this "profit," they might fail to recognize the extra time with their family that more money could buy. Someone might value their religion to the point that they fail to consider the church's need for funding, causing the church to falter.

These errors affect our lives, but they also change the ability to use Profit Motive as a way to forecast and understand the actions of others.

A Personal Look: A Day of Using the Profit-Motive View

Waking up in the morning I look at my phone and pull up a few websites. First, I pull up the Drudge Report to see the breaking news from overnight, and then I can see the articles and the headlines Matt Drudge has laid out for the day. The whole time in the back of my head I know that Drudge leans right, that his niche is writing attractive headlines that drive a narrative. I like trying to figure out the narrative that he is attempting to communicate, because on an hour by hour or even a day by day basis, he can be tricky to pin down. But, knowing that Drudge is right-leaning, that he rewrites headlines to make them snappier, more clickable, and to tell a story, I can enjoy the rest of the site. Drudge has an eye for news, and other media have picked up on that and crib from his site and headline sculpting. His site is simple, quick, and easy to fully browse and take in. (He has not updated the site's design since 1997.) I get the profit of reduced time reading morning news, Drudge makes profits from showing me ads, and a few lucky journalists get hundreds of thousands, or millions, of extra reads if Matt picked their story.

I then shower. I use an organic soap. Why? I pay more for my soap because of an accident, genetics, and Profit Motive. The soap that I use is the one that we use on our three kids. The other baby/child soaps have more chemicals in them. That isn't necessarily bad. They provide other things that parents like, such as bubbles to make them feel like are doing a better cleaning, scents that they associate with how a baby smells, and a trusted brand name. The other companies have marketed themselves well, so we first used their soaps for bathing our children. However, after the chemicals they used affected our kids' skin we switched brands; their skin and hair became so much better that both my wife and I started using the new organic brand as well. So, I have lost a little cash, but my kids have healthier skin and we all have cleaner hair. The other company has the lion's share of the market because they are marketing to that lion's share and giving them what they want.

After the shower I head downstairs where my family is usually already awake and eating breakfast. On the TV is *The Today Show*. While I eat my breakfast, there is usually a segment on about cooking, home improvement, or a great deal on something. These are all segments geared toward providing me, my family, and the other viewers enough value that we will tune back in tomorrow. The guests interviewed for those segments are on the show for another reason, though. They want to sell you more of the value that they just provided. It is a game of exchanging value for time.

I then walk my daughter to school. I lose some time from my work day, but only a few minutes, and I get to spend ten minutes with my daughter before the working day even starts. I can only hope that she gets something out of it, but these ten minutes are one of the reasons that I value running my own business. It would be nearly impossible to walk her to school and get to any job in the city by 9:00 a.m. Fortunately, I don't have to be at work at nine o'clock. Unfortunately, that means that I take on a higher level of risk and that I often work what would be considered "odd" or "long" hours.

I then drive to work. My office is in Springfield, VA, so I don't have to drive fully into DC every day, but even when I do I don't take the Metro. I no longer live within walking distance of a station, so if I took the Metro I would have to drive to the station, pay to park, park, walk to the platform, pay to ride, and then sit or stand for thirty to forty minutes with a bunch of other people on their daily migration. I also don't take the train, which is closer to my house in the suburbs than the Metro, for largely the same reasons. However, the biggest problem with the train is that with fewer time options it doesn't provide the flexibility that my schedule requires. Also, since I have decided to forego the other options, I have also decided against picking up sluggers. I pay more for my commute, but I get to enjoy the time to myself and benefit from the time thinking.

When I get to work, I check emails, I set up my calendar, and then I go through my clients one by one to assess their needs and the strategy to maximize their profit from working with my company, so that they continue to work with me. To do this I provide them with two types of services. First, I give them frequent general updates. These small, but frequent, actions let the client know that we are active on their behalf. Second, I work on creating and implementing deeper strategic actions. These provide the long-run value that help distinguish my company from others. By attempting to focus on what my client needs, I am focusing on their Profit Motive for working with me.

This one goes a bit deeper though. The person that I work with as my "client" is sometimes the business owner who just wants value, but a lot of times it is someone who reports to a manager and is part of a bigger organization and they normally have different Profit Motives from the owner of a company. That person wants value, but they may also benefit from more updates, more actions, and perhaps being involved more with certain projects. It can give them the opportunity to brag about how much work their subcontractor is doing. The owner of business is likely focused on just his business, but someone under the boss has their own Profit Motives, and if you can identify those you might then be able to enjoy a more lucrative relationship with that client.

Moving to lunch, I am not as productive as some of my friends, but eating is something that everyone does, which makes it easy to share someone's time. As my friend Ike Brannon says, "You should never eat lunch at your desk or alone." The point that he is making is that lunch time is an easy time to exchange, and perhaps multiply, value with someone else. If I do eat lunch alone or in my office, I do try to scold myself and remind myself that I need to get out. However, now that I spend more time in Springfield, VA, which is fifteen to twenty minutes away from the city, a lunch might cost me an additional forty minutes (let alone how much time it would take to park), which means that I also now weigh whether the extra time is worth it or not. (Profit Man would likely always say that it is worth it.)

Post-lunch is different from day to day, but on Wednesdays I do a lot of media. Before I go on air, I focus on what my message is, what their message is, and what my role is going to be in the discussion. If I am on a friendly network, my role is normally to provide supporting numbers, data points, and history. If I am on an antagonistic network, my role is to counter their claims. However, this opposition can take on two forms and it depends on the network and the message. Since I do Thom Hartman and his radio and TV shows a lot, I generally directly address his talking points because he wants to get into a more substantive debate. However, on other shows it is better, or more acceptable, to stick with top-level messaging points because getting into the weeds won't help your argument over the course of a five-minute segment. Focusing on these different questions helps clean up my message and helps secure an invitation to return.

I haven't always been very disciplined about focusing on the Profit Motive of the hosts. In fact, on one show that was supposed to be friendly, I was repeatedly antagonistic. My arguments weren't caustic, ad-hominem, or made-up, but they didn't make the host look good. So, I haven't been called back to participate on that show. The host is pursuing his own Profit Motive, and losing a debate to a guest wasn't a part of that equation.

Once I am done I try to head home for dinner with my kids. Sometimes I make it, and sometimes I don't, but more often than not I am back in time to play with them for a few minutes and help put them to bed. Again, this is a result of having my own business because they eat pretty early. I also lose some desk time at my office, or I must cut my meeting time short one or two slots. But the time with family is important, so I do it.

After dinner, play time, and baths, the kids are put to bed, and then I get to spend time with my wife. Since I often short the normal workday at both the beginning and at the end, I often have more work that I need to do, but if we didn't spend this time together, we wouldn't get almost any time to ourselves. Not to mention the fact that she needs this time. She has often been just with the kids all day, so talking about things, making decisions, or just watching TV with a grown-up is what she needs and wants.

One decision that we had to discuss during this time together, that had an interesting amount of Profit Motive in it, was whether or not we would send our girls to church camp. Church camps, I didn't know before this time, are amazingly inexpensive. They are so cheap that they are basically free. I think that the cost of the camp is mainly to pay for the cost of supplies and that all the labor and facility space is donated. If we weren't thinking about Profit Motive, we might just assume that this is a great deal and jump at the opportunity. However, we talked about why the price was so low. We understood the church was recruiting our family through our kids and what that meant. In the end, both my wife and I were fine with the church's Profit Motives, and we actually sent our kids to two different church camps. Our main Profit Motive was inexpensive child care, and letting our daughters learn about the two different churches was something that we were all right with—at least while they were five and three (the one-year-old was too young to attend yet). On the other side, the church was making a great investment. They were only asking their parishioners for time, they already have the space, and for that the church gets to market to area families. It is another win-win.

After we talked and watched TV, my wife went to bed, and that is when I finish my work, which is more reading, more emails, more thinking, and more writing. Sometimes I make it to the gym after that, but usually it is time for me to go to bed and soon start it all over the next day.

Life moves by quickly, but recognizing my own Profit Motives helps me understand and leverage those of others more readily.

Leveraging Profit Motives

"We are only just beginning to understand the power of love because we are just beginning to understand the weakness of force and aggression."

—B.F. Skinner, *Walden Two*

The way to use Profit Motive thinking isn't to yell at someone, point at them, and say, "You are just trying to make a profit!" It isn't to slap someone's hands when they are trying to make a profit from working with you. It isn't to exclaim in outrage that someone is trying to profit from their actions. There is a possibility that these methods might work in the short-run, they might work once, and they might work in certain circumstances. However, the way that profit motivates us should be assumed.

Like water flowing downhill, the motivation to profit can't be stopped, but it can be directed and leveraged.

One way to leverage profit motives is to short-circuit profit-based motivations. Hours and hours of our lives are taken up by people pursuing a profit that you aren't going to give them. For instance, a lot of chain restaurant waiters have scripts that they are supposed to go through in order to help out the sales of the restaurant, like mentioning two apps, offering a liquor upgrade, selling the chicken special, etc. There might be some people who want all of this information, but my wife and I don't want a commercial at our table. So we just let the waiter know that we know what we want, and that we aren't a secret shopper. We have relieved the waiter from his motivation to check boxes off of a secret shopper's list, and we have given him Profit Motive to focus on the service instead of the sales.

A tougher one, but another time waster, is to end the motivation of people to talk on a conference call just to let people know that they are there. These people take hours out of our days each year, but they are just attempting to show that they provide value. This fills up needless or pointless conference calls with even more needless or pointless statements. The way to end this is fairly simple: have everyone announce their attendance, and then only ask if people have questions. The only questions that you are likely to get are from people who don't understand something or from those that have a concern, but it is hard to ask a question merely because someone wants others to know that they are there. The potential profit from speaking has been lowered by this introduction and the barrier to entry into the conversation is higher.

The thing about having Profit Motive is that its effects are small, but its effects are persistent. It is the constant pressure that we can use to work the world toward our advantage. This is one of the reasons that I think that something like goal setting, or the idea of thinking about your goals and desires (like in the book *The Secret*), are more effective once you recognize the ways that Profit

Motive works. If your goal is a new house, and you make your Profit Motive geared toward getting that new house, then other decisions that you make will change. You will be moving the constant pressure of your Profit Motive toward that new house. When you get a raise, you will have an idea of how much more you need to make. When you go out to dinner, you will have a reason to spend less to have less profit in entertainment, more profit from saving. If you are in a bad relationship and one that makes it harder to reach your goal of a burying new house, you are more likely to end the relationship (or question your goal of the house). The same is all true if you want a happier family, a new car, a better job, more time to spend on your hobby, or anything else that you value.

Altruism vs. Cash Motivation

We have gone over this again and again, but profit isn't always cash or riches. Profit, in the frame of Profit Motive is what you make it. You can be altruistic and the people that you deal with can be altruistic. Or, you can be motivated by cash and the people that you deal with can also be motivated by cash.

The true multiplier that can be gained from understanding a Profit Motive is the idea that you might be altruistic, and you might need to engage someone that is motivated by cash. Their motivation doesn't change yours; their motivation and your understanding their motivation might help you be more altruistic.

Let's take another example of churches again. If you are raising money for your church, you might have to work with a fundraiser. If you do, there are several options. One way might be to find a member of the church to do the fundraising for free. That sounds great. But another way would be to find a for-profit fundraiser. This person raising money for a living might know what grant money is available. They might know a lot of wealthy people. They also might just be good at running a capital campaign.

Paying someone, and acknowledging and allowing them to profit, might help the church to raise a large percentage more than if the same project was run by a volunteer.

Another example of this has become a large part of US culture: Girl Scout Cookie sales. This amazing idea "provides" a lot of funding for the Girl Scouts in addition to teaching the girls about entrepreneurship and sales in a way that no other program could. Of course, that is because they are actually the seasonal sales arms of the for-profit bakery that makes the cookies. The relationship of everyone involved is built on the profit of the other one. We have a nonprofit working with a for-profit and everyone loves it. From the little girls selling the cookies, to the parents assisting them, to the people baking the cookies, and of course the people eating the cookies, the relationships just work out.

The people eating the cookies are able to donate to a charity, teach a new generation about sales and entrepreneurship, and eat cookies that provide an almost equivalent value as the donation. The bakery that makes the cookies makes a ton of money from the Girl Scouts. But in order to make that money they have had to rely on a distribution method that is slow and disorganized, and that method doesn't get much better year-to-year. However, they rely on this slow method because at the other end is a relatively large and motivated labor force that is able to present the cookies to houses that can't be marketed to under normal circumstances. Heck, in the area that I live door-to-door sales are against the rules, but the Girl Scouts have an exemption that allows them to solicit. It is a market coup that no other cookie seller has. The parents get help paying for Girl Scout adventures that would likely have to pay for anyway, all the while teaching their kids the value of hard work and sales. And the girls learn the invaluable lesson of sales, with a beloved product, and earn money that helps support their troop and the Girl Scouts in general.

It is an amazing program, but it also has its problems. The cookie selling operation is not as organized as it could or should be. Systems are disconnected, forms don't match up, and it is obvious that Band-Aids have been applied over Band-Aids to keep the system functioning. The best information and supplies are of course provided by the bakery, but the supplies that come from the Girl Scouts often are hard to use and are cumbersome. Of course, looking at the system through the lens of Profit Motive, the Girl Scouts must not be investing much into the program. They have free labor, and they are using it. However, how much more could be done if they cleaned up their end. Could they make more?

I think they could, and I think that they should. But, they aren't likely to unless somebody takes leadership of the Girl Scouts with a Profit Motive to grow the program by applying more business strategy.

The right answer when looking at altruism vs. cash profit is that it doesn't matter. What matters is recognizing the differing motivation and figuring out how to make those work together.

Profiting from This Book

My hope is that you can use this book to profit. My hope is that you can take these ideas and make your company bigger, hire more people, spend more time with your family, or build a better community. Profit Motive doesn't make you richer; it helps you understand how to get richer. Profit Motive is the key, but you have to turn it into profit yourself.

We started with a thought experiment. Let's end with one too: If a person wants to profit, is it best to read a book, write a book, or sell a book?

Interviews with Business, Commmunity, and Media Leaders Held with the Author for This Book

I am grateful to the following business leaders for engaging in the interviews I conducted for this book. They really help tell the story and even further inspired me in the writing of the manuscript. All information below is accurate according to the author's records.

Nicholas Buchanan, phone interview on September 23, 2015, with follow-up emails and phone calls

Sandra Bond Chapman, PhD, email interview, December 20, 2016, with follow-up emails and phone calls

Ron Devine, in person interview, December 5, 2016 with follow-up emails

Godwin Dixon, email interview, December 20, 2016 with follow-up phone calls and emails.

Thom Hartman, in person interview, October 7, 2016 with follow-up emails.

Doug Humphrey, in person interview, December 16, 2016 with follow-up emails

Jay Kempton, email interview, December 22, 2016 with follow-up emails and phone calls

Dave Mohel, phone interview, October 25, 2016 with follow-up emails and phone calls

Terry Neese, phone call interview, January 15, 2016 with follow-up emails and phone calls

Christina Norris, email interview, December 15, 2016 with follow-up emails.

Rev. Molly Simpson, United Methodist clergy, phone call interview, January 17, 2016 with follow up emails

Dr. Keith Smith, email interview, January 2, 2016 with follow-up emails and phone calls

Andrea Sauer, in person interview, October 2, 2017 with follow-up emails

Notes

1. "http://www.datacenterknowledge.com/the-facebook-data-center-faq/,"
   16 September 2016. [Online]. [Accessed 15 October 2016].

2. Ayn Rand, *Virture of Selfishness: A New Concept of Egoism* (New York: Penguin, 1964).

3. Richard Thaler and Cass Sunstein, *Nudge: Improving Decisions About Health, Wealth, and Happiness* (Penguin Books, 2009).

4. Ryan Young and Iain Murry, "The Rising Tide: Answering the Right Questions in the Inequality Debate," 2016.

5. Ron Chernow, *Titan: The Life of John D. Rockefeller, Sr.* (Vintage Press, 2004).

6. Chris Isidore, "Tesla Got 200,000 orders for the Model 3 in the First Day." "http://money.cnn.com/2016/04/01/news/companies/tesla-model-3-stock-price/," 1 April 2016. [Online]. [Accessed 2016].

7. Jerry Hirsch, "Elon Musk's Growing Empire Is Fueled by $4.9 Billion in Government Subsidies," *Los Angeles Times*, 30 May 2015.

8. Laura Tillman, "Billionaire Musk Gets Brownsville to Pay for SpaceX," *Bloomberg Markets*, 12 February 2014.

9. Timothy P. Carney, "Elon Musk's Rocket Company Gets Subsidies from U.S. and France," *Washington Examiner*, 4 April 2014.

10. Kelefa Sanneh, "Everyone Hates Martin Shkreli. Everyone Is Missing the Point," *The New Yorker* "http://www.newyorker.com/culture/cultural-comment/everyone-hates-martin-shkreli-everyone-is-missing-the-point," 15 February 2016. [Online]. [Accessed 2016].

11. David Dayen, "Why Martin Shreli Has Been a Godsend to the Drug Industry," The Fiscal Times. "http://www.thefiscaltimes.com/Columns/2016/02/04/Why-Martin-Shkreli-Has-Been-Godsend-Drug-Industry," 4th February 2016. [Online]. [Accessed 2016].

12. Robert Reich, "Martin Shkreli Is Just a Product of American Capitalism," Salon.com. "http://www.salon.com/2015/12/23/robert_reich_martin_shkreli_is_just_a_product_of_american_capitalism_partner/," 23 December 2015. [Online]. [Accessed 2016].

13. Drugs.com, "https://www.drugs.com/pro/daraprim.html," 2016. [Online]. [Accessed 2016].

14. Matthew Iglesias, "Sandy Price Gouging: Anti-Gouging Laws Make Natural Disasters Worse," Slate.com. "http://www.slate.com/articles/business/moneybox/2012/10/sandy _price_gouging_anti_gouging_laws_make_natural_disasters_worse. html," 30 October 2012. [Online]. [Accessed 2016].

15. Council of Econims Advisers (brief), "Gender Pay Gap: Recent Trends and Explanations," 2015.

16. US Bureau of Labor Statistics, "https://www.bls.gov/opub/ted/2013/ted _20130806.htm," 6 August 2013. [Online]. [Accessed 11 September 2017].

17. Ekaterina Jardim, Mark C. Long, Robert Plotnick, Emma van Inwegan, Jacob Vigdor, Hialry Wething, "Minimum Wage Increases, Wages, and Low-Wage Employment: Evidence from Seattle," National Bureau of Economic Research, Cambridge, 2017.

18. Ryan Young and Iain Murray, "The Rising Tide: Answering the Right Questions in the Inequality Debate ssrn.2789023," May 25, 2016.

19. Center for Responsive Politics, "https://www.opensecrets.org/lobby/," [Online]. [Accessed December 2016].

20. Center for Responsive Politics, OpenSecrets.org. "https://www.opensecrets.org/lobby/," [Online]. [Accessed 2016].

21. "The 2016 Annual Report of the Board of Trustees, Federal Old-Age and Survivors Insurance and Federal Disability Insurance Trust Funds," U.S. Government Publishing Office, Washington, 2016.

22. United States Elections Project.org., "Voter Turnout Demographics." "http://www.electproject.org/home/voter-turnout/demographics," 2016. [Online]. [Accessed 2016].

23. Anyau and Andrew Mayersohn, "Donor Demographics, Old White Guys Edition, Part III, OpenSecrets.org. https://www.opensecrets.org/news/2015/06/donor-demographics-old -white-guys-edition-part-i/," 11th June 2015. [Online]. [Accessed 2016].

24. Chares Krauthammer, "An Embarrassment of Liars, Whiners and Trite Politicians," *Chicago Tribune,* 28th October 1994.

25. David Mohel, President of Blue Skin Solution, interviewee. [author interview], 25 October 2016.

26. Kenneth P. Vogel and Lucy McCalmont, "Top Radio Talkers Sell Endorsements," Politico. "http://www.politico.com/story/2011/06/top-radio-talkers-sell -endorsements-056997," 6 June 2011. [Online]. [Accessed 2016].

27. Glen Beck, "Glen Beck: Big Auto Bailout?," "http://www.glennbeck.com/content/articles/article/198/18002/," 10 October 2013. [Online]. [Accessed 18 October 2016].

28. Thom Hartmann, interviewee, [author interview]. 16 October 2016.

29. Timothy Groseclose and Jeffrey Milyo, "A Measure of Media Bias," *The Quarterly Journal of Economics, 120*, pp. 1191-1237, 2005.

30. D. K. Smith, Interviewee, [author interview]. 2 January 2017.

31. Uri Gneezy and John List, *The Why Axis: Hidden Motives and the Undiscovered Economics of Everyday Life* (PublicAffairs, 2013).

32. Joe Pinsker, "Finland, Home of the $103,000 Speeding Ticket," *The Atlantic*, 12 March 2015. [Online]. Available: http://www.theatlantic.com/business/archive/2015/03/finland-home-of-the-103000-speeding-ticket/387484/.

33. Benjamin D. Sommers, MD, PhD, and Arnold M. Epstein, "Medicaid Expansion—The Soft Underbelly of Health Care Reform?," *The New England Journal of Medicine*, 2010.

34. Katherine Baicker, et al., "The Oregon Experiment—Effects of Medicaid on Clinical Outcomes," *The New England Journal of Medicine*, 2013.

35. Steven R. Covey, *The 7 Habits of Highly Effective People* (Free Press, USA, 2004).

36. B. F. Skinner, *Science and Human Behavior* (New York: Macmillan, 1953).

Index

About the Author

Photograph © Max Taylor

Charles Sauer is an economist, policy specialist, and writer. He has spent time on Capitol Hill working for the Chairman of the Senate Finance Committee, and he has worked for a governor on tax, immigration, and labor issues; and was Deputy Legislative Director for an academic think tank focusing on tax, finance, and health care. Charles runs the Market Institute, is a founder of the Savings and Retirement Foundation, a CoDirector of the Inventor's Project, and host of the Prosperity Caucus.

Charles is a frequent contributor to *The Weekly Standard*, a *Washington Examiner* contributor, and has written for *Forbes, Investor's Business Daily,* Entrepreneur.com, *The Washington Times, The Daily Caller,* and numerous other publications. Additionally, Charles Sauer appears frequently on One America News as well as *The Big Picture with Thom Hartmann*, and the *Thom Hartmann Radio Program*.

In addition to his life in politics and writing, Charles enjoys spending time with his family. He is married to Andrea Sauer, the love of his life and the supporter that he credits for being able to freely pursue his dreams, and they have three beautiful daughters: Anna, Madonna, and Charlotte.